SHAKESPEARE THE CRAFTSMAN

SHAKESPEARE
THE CRAFTSMAN

THE CLARK LECTURES
1968

By

M. C. Bradbrook, Litt.D.
*Mistress of Girton College and
Professor of English Literature,
Cambridge University*

BARNES & NOBLE, Inc.
NEW YORK
PUBLISHERS & BOOKSELLERS SINCE 1873

PUBLISHED IN GREAT BRITAIN BY
Chatto & Windus Ltd.
42 William IV Street
London, W.C.2
★
First published in the United States of America, 1969
by Barnes & Noble, Inc.

CLARK LECTURES

SIXTY YEARS AGO

A number of us used to go to the Clark Lectures at Trinity College which the wives and daughters of the faculties at the various colleges were permitted to attend should they wish. We had to climb a staircase at Trinity to reach the lecture room, and at the top of the stairs was stationed a gyp whose duty was to shout repeatedly 'Girton and Newnham to the right! Ladies to the left! Girton and Newnham to the right! Ladies to the left!' This left us under no illusions as to our position in the gyp world.

E. Millicent Sowerby (Girton 1908-1912)
Rare Books and Rare People (1967)

The Council of Trinity College, by inviting me to deliver the Clark Lectures for 1968 gave an opportunity to honour the memory of a great Shakespearean editor, for which my most grateful thanks are due.

Chapter Two is based on material given at Sydney as the Kathleen Robinson lecture in 1967. Chapter Eight formed my inaugural lecture at Cambridge in February 1966, and I am obliged to the Syndics of the Cambridge University Press for leave to reproduce it here.

My secretary Mrs Rignold has given me invaluable help in preparing the book.

CONTENTS

Chapter		Page
I	Introduction	I
II	A Craftsman's Theatre: from Mystery to Chronicle	4
	i. From Pageant to Play	4
	ii. The English History Play . . .	11
	iii. Shakespeare's Epilogue. . . .	22
III	Shakespeare's Gild of Players . . .	27
	i. James Burbage, Founder of the Theatre	27
	ii. Shakespeare's Choice	30
	iii. Shews at the Globe	38
	iv. The Later History	42
IV	The New Clown: *Twelfth Night* . .	49
	i. Robert Armin	49
	ii. *Twelfth Night* and the Reign of Fortune	57
	iii. Armin's Later Career	67
V	Royal Command: *The Merry Wives of Windsor*	75
VI	The Lives of the Noble Romans: *Julius Caesar* and Other Roman Histories .	97
VII	Old Things Made New: *Hamlet, Prince of Denmark*.	122
	i. The Older *Hamlet* Plays . . .	122
	ii. The New Revenge Plays . . .	126
	iii. The Later *Hamlets*	139
VIII	Blackfriars: The Pageant of *Timon of Athens*	144
	Notes.	169

PLATES
(between pages 30-31)

A Wheel of Fortune, *Memento Mori*, and Tree of Life

London, the earliest map
(By courtesy of the Trustees of the British Museum)

The Wheel of Fortune (Henry VIII and Edward VI)
(By courtesy of the Trustees of the National Portrait Gallery)

CHAPTER I

INTRODUCTION

CRAFTSMANSHIP in Elizabethan drama developed with the opportunities given when the professional theatre of London established a demand. From 1576, when the first theatre was opened by James Burbage, to 1594, when he refounded the Lord Chamberlain's Men with Shakespeare as their poet, the search for craft forms proceeded. By the mid 1590s stability had emerged as new traditions were founded; hack writers were turning out plays in a fortnight or three weeks.

Having already considered the social history of the actors in *The Rise of the Common Player*, my first purpose is to show the descent of Shakespeare's art from the popular medieval tradition, especially from the religious drama of the craft cycles. In this I follow other students of the medieval and renaissance stage, who have filled out the dramatic tradition, as distinct from the merely literary one.

Shakespeare's work blossomed suddenly into the full greatness that sets him so splendidly apart from all his contemporaries. The years between 1599 and 1602 appear to have seen not only the four masterpieces which I have dealt with in four later chapters of the book, but possibly other plays, such as *Henry V* and *Troilus and Cressida*. After a period in which almost alone, except for Henslowe's hacks, he had been writing steadily, he had been joined by younger men; the fruitful interaction of their work and his, the stimulus of moving to a new playhouse of which he was part-owner, and the immediate chances which those years afforded brought a rich variety of 'tragedy, comedy, history, pastoral', culminating in *Hamlet*.

In this play, where the actors themselves appear on stage, the actor-audience relationship is adjusted on a level as firm as that of the old popular craft plays; the craft-mystery of the actor itself becomes both ground and edifice of the new drama.

Hamlet initiates the great decade of Jonson, Chapman, Tourneur, Webster, Middleton; its direct effect can be registered in the work of the latest craftsman of the pre-Restoration stage, Dick Brome, who served his 'prentice-ship with the King's Men.

Tradition was transformed by a new and self-conscious art, that was yet free of petty theoretic prescriptions or narrowly didactic aims, evincing the spontaneous power that makes for growth and that has made *Hamlet* itself the basis for many later dramatic experiments.

In the course of the survey, leading up to and then concentrating on this very brief period, I have used one or two specific themes; for example, the stage monsters shew how a spectacular stage was incorporated, through the development of poetic imagery, into an imaginative world. The Goddess Fortune, motive force and emblem of medieval tragedy, is first transformed into a more pragmatic notion of Fortune as Occasion, and finally incarnate in human characters, as they interact on one another.

In the rich tapestry of Shakespeare's designs, lines of development should not be separated out too sharply. I have tried to subordinate tracing patterns and trends of craftsmanship to following the complexity of the living art. The chief explanation of Shakespeare's variety may be his sensitive response to specific demands made upon him; if the illustrations seem dense and close-packed, so was the full and crowded life, the full and crowded art of those London years.

(The last chapter, which was originally a separate lecture treats of the last phase of Shakespeare's craftsmanship, when his company moved to the new indoor theatre at Blackfriars; it is in the nature of an epilogue.)

My second purpose therefore is to relate Shakespeare's craftsmanship to the immediate situation which gave rise to his individual plays: a new actor, a special occasion, a new stage. Hence the significance of studying in detail such a short space of time. The earlier work and the literary affiliations I have treated in *Shakespeare and Elizabethan Poetry*; here, in addition to greater concentration, there is also a more technical approach.

This, I hope, should contribute to the third and paramount purpose of this study, the better understanding of the plays themselves.

CHAPTER II

A CRAFTSMAN'S THEATRE:
FROM MYSTERY TO CHRONICLE

Action is eloquent and the eyes of the ignorant
More learned than the ears. (*Coriolanus*, 3.1.76-7)

i. From Pageant to Play

C. S. LEWIS described Spenser's great epic as 'a
verbalization of pageant . . . we are meant to *look* and
see the *shews* it presents'.[1] This ancient mode (as Lewis
goes on to remark) is not so much a comment on life as
life itself translated into another form. Shews carry the
embodied emotions of society—they generate the dynamics of its cohesion.

When Robert d'Artois bore into the feast of King
Edward I the heron he had taken with his falcon along
the river, and challenged the King by presenting this
cowardly and solitary bird, the King vowed to invade
France and regain his lost right. As Robert presented the
heron to each, vassals in turn swore on the heron to follow;
lastly the Queen vowed that the child she carried should
be born on French soil. The Vows of the Heron turned
a ceremonious feast into an army camp and themselves
furnished matter for a poem.

That shaken mood which fell on the feasters when the
Green Knight rode into Arthur's Hall belongs to the
ceremonies both of life and of drama, as defined by a
modern master of interludes:

> The sudden appearance of a fabricated Being, made of wood
> and cloth, entirely invented, corresponding to nothing, yet dis-
> quieting by nature, capable of re-introducing on the stage a little
> breath of that great metaphysical fear which is at the root of all
> ancient theatre.

Elsewhere, Artaud spoke of 'the theatre's excruciating
magic relation to reality and danger'.[2]

4

Four hundred years of pageant lay behind the plays of Shakespeare, whose work is so much more than a verbalization. To recover what a previous Clark Lecturer termed 'the visual meaning', we must follow those processions whose movements are felt in the empathy of tragic poetry. What remains for evocation, the numinous awe of rhythmic patterns, survives in Shakespeare, though the embodied action may be replaced by imaginative sequences.

The six pageants of *Macbeth*, three seen and three unseen, implement the magic relation of a play originally written for a king in whose person some of the prophecies were fulfilled.

The ghastly pageant of war, represented by the Bleeding Sergeant, finds Macbeth an artificer in 'the royal Occupation':

> Nothing afeard of that which thou didst make,
> Strange images of death. (1.3.96-7)

When Banquo's fulfilment of his vassal's oath confronts Macbeth at his coronation feast with a new *pageant* of death, the King appeals for more monstrous, less accusing forms:

> Approach thou like the rugged Russian bear,
> The arm'd rhinoceros or the Hyrcan tyger,
> Take any shape but that. (3.5.100-2)

Banquo next acts as Presenter to a coronation pageant of shadowy kings, who, succeeding the riddling homage of the witches in their cavern, pace slowly by Macbeth to 'shew his eyes and grieve his heart'. The measured rhythm sinks into his mind; and it re-echoes when the cry of wailing women, with the word of his wife's death, destroys hope of any posterity for him.

> Tomorrow,
> and tomorrow,
> and tomorrow
> Creeps in this petty pace from day to day.... (5.5.19-20)

By some dark sympathy the candle we have seen in the dead woman's hand now flickers through Macbeth's imagination, lighting a procession of fools in a Dance of Death. The Presenter—an Idiot—stands by, like the Orator in the *The Chairs*, telling the vacant tale.

But we have met another invisible Dance of Death— admitted to the Castle of Macbeth by a drunken fool. Who is the climactic unnamed Figure whose presence chills and sobers the Porter—Death or the Devil?

> Faith, here's an English tailor come hither for stealing out of a French hose. Come in, tailor, here you may roast your goose. . . . Knock, knock, knock, never at quiet. . . . *What* are you? . . . . But this place is too cold for hell. . . .   (2.3.16-20)

The game had turned into something else.

Of recent years, stage revivals and social historians have reinterpreted medieval pageants (I will mention only the work of Wickham, Hardison and Kolve),[3] and the great authorities of E. K. Chambers and Karl Young have been drastically questioned, till now they receive only the quali-fied kind of homage accorded to Frazer's *Golden Bough* and other scholarly monuments of a generation that has receded into the past. Their indifference to living theatre, and even to the behavioural aspects of religious observance governed their presuppositions and distorted their inter-pretation of the documents they were the first to assemble and present.

The principle of medieval pageantry is a sacramental one, the principle of Transformation. In game or play creatures appearing to come from a world beyond the world erupt to meet the audience. By participating in the play, the audience enter into relation with that other world. This effects a change in the nature of their relationship with the total order of creatures, which though only in game, may have sacramental effects.

Processions, pageants, triumphs draw power from an ordered movement because such order prefigures and harmonizes with the order of the universe. As St Gregory the Great said 'High things are joined to low, earthly to heavenly, and one thing is made of visible and invisible'.

A very early craftsman's play, written for a May Game

in 1262, shews the townsfolk of Arras moving in and out of a supernatural order in the streets of their own town. Hellequin and three Fairy Queens arrive, in what has been described as a ritual game for Queen Mab and the midwives' gild of Arras.[4]

The theory that plays began in the church does not fit the facts; but in England the combination of clerics with town gilds united the oldest and youngest cohesive forces of late medieval society. At least two hundred years' pageantry lay behind the great English gild cycles, and two hundred years more of the gild cycles lay behind the Elizabethan theatre. The social implications of this drama, in actor-audience relations, is of more deep significance than its form.

York, Coventry, Lincoln, Norwich, enacted Cosmic Histories from the Creation to the Last Judgment within a grand framework which, as Kolve has shewn, was based on the Seven Ages of the World. World Histories, where the actors themselves held a place, presented the macrocosm, the total creation as it evolved under God's providential plan. Those episodes, and only those, which shew the continuity and balance of the Seven Ages were selected. A pattern was imposed on history, cutting out such dramatic stories as David and Bathsheba. Prefiguration linked the series (the Sacrifice of Isaac symbolizing the Sacrifice of Christ, for example); each episode turns on the two central acts—'A man, a maiden and a tree'. 'Christ's cross and Adam's tree stood in one place', said Herbert; round these two episodes the structure could be contracted or expanded. No need to play the whole series every year. Parts served to exemplify the Eternal Order underlying Creation, built into the very structure of things. I myself have participated in a ritual of transformation, at Easter week processions in the little Spanish town of Santa Cruz de Tenerife.

Every day in Holy Week, the plaza filled with the Bus Conductors' Band, the Red Cross Band, and the village children. Dressed in Biblical costumes, and waving palms, they triumphed on Palm Sunday. The church images were carried round the port with all the pomp that a poor community could manage; first an evangelist writing in his book, then Simon of Cyrene, maybe, in the local fisher's garb, with a cross of rough wood. As the dawn of Friday broke, to the sound of high wailing a great silver crucifix was borne out, as the village cocks began to crow. On Easter Eve, no bands and no lights; only the image of the Virgin in black, carried by the children to a mournful song. But as night drew on, a crowd assembled, and the strange staccato chant they raised seemed both menacing and pagan. Then, at midnight, as the bells rang, everyone rushed off into the narrow streets, crying 'He's got up!' to look for a tavern.

I wondered, next morning what could succeed; possibly, as in Seville, just cockfighting, but quite early the bands and the children and the crowd were back again. Before the church door appeared a red baldachin, borne by four priests—the very kind so often shewn in Elizabethan royal pictures. Out stepped another priest and in his hands a gold disk, with the Host. Men knelt on the stones, women threw roses from the balconies, the bands struck up, the bells all clashed. No image; but Himself in person. The change of mode produced the most purely dramatic *coup de théâtre*—to put it profanely. Now this was what happened at the end of the gild cycles, which were performed at the feast of Corpus Christi. The shock of removal from past and future to here, now and always, from play and game to truth, leads everyone into the Play beyond the Play.[5]

Clerics like John Mirk defended the use of images because without them 'there be many thousand of pepul that cold not imagine in her hart how Christ was done on rod, but as they lern hit be syght of images and payntours'. But even in the fourteenth century a new mood appeared. Woe worth the child of a hundred years, exclaimed the Wycliffite preacher in denouncing plays as mere folly and offensive to true majesty.

Gild plays unified all levels of society; the Chester play quotes in Latin 'for clerkes here present'; Henry V, Margaret of Anjou, Richard III, all saw the Coventry plays;

Henry VII saw them twice. Civic pageants blended religious and secular history. Shakespeare may have seen the Coventry shew of the English triumph over the Danes; he was eleven years old when it was played at Kenilworth before Queen Elizabeth.

The many-headed monster

The gild play offered one of the more important social embodiments of Professor Ullmann's twin theses of political society in the Middle Ages—hierarchy, *auctoritas*, or community, citizenship; subjection to order, or equality in enterprises.[6] Some gilds would seem to have been founded largely in order to produce a play.

London craft gilds seem to have preferred the pomp of royal entries or coronations and Shakespeare could rely on the deep sense of community and hierarchy evoked, in his latest play, *The Famous Life of King Henry VIII*, after much of the tradition had withered.

From the mid-fifteenth century, as the researches of Giles Dawson have recently disclosed,[7] the local records of Kent yield at least twice as much playing activity as had previously been known. Such audiences were already part of the local play before it began, since production had involved them. In New Romney, nine years before Shakespeare was born, townspeople met to decide what each man

'Time hath, my lord, a wallet at his back'

should give towards their passion play. 'Mr Holden buildeth heaven'; John Davy promised help with his wain; many more offered three days' work and small sums of money, for which they were promised repayment. The play was given on a series of scaffolds and places set up for Pilate and the princes, for Annas and the torturers, for the Pharisees, Herod, a Cave or Tomb, and Hell.

Under the shock of the Reformation and its militant nationalism, images, symbols, and conflict systems of the older cycles were transferred to the cyclic history of the English people for which preparation had already begun.

The history of the Canterbury pageant of St Thomas à Becket shews the transition from sacred pageantry to playing. Brought out annually from the priory of St Sepulchre's, this pageant witnessed to the craftsmanship of its builders rather than their dramatic skill. The star performer was a mechanical angel that flapped its wings when a vice was screwed; for which the operator received twopence. Small boys played the knights or tormentors with evident zeal, as the image of St Thomas required frequent repairs, especially repainting of the head; so did the knights' leather harness.

Suddenly in 1537 the saint was decanonized, and we hear of 'Bishop Becket's pageant', which within four years is replaced by a play.

In matters of public ceremonial, the dramatic flair of Henry VIII and Elizabeth allowed the transference of many sacred types and images to themselves such as Joshua, David, Moses, Deborah, Judith and the Virgin Mary.

In the royal theatre erected for Henry VIII at Greenwich in 1527, Hans Holbein painted a ceiling that shewed the earth surrounded by the sea, and also, designed by the Astronomer Royal, a Heaven of Stars.[8] Total Creation was still contained within the play; there was order among the spectators, for the Venetian ambassador wrote of them circling two trees of peace, bearing the emblems of English and French chivalric orders, St Michael and St George. Hierarchy, in Ullmann's term, prevailed over Community; a little debate on Love and Riches by the choirboys provided an interlude to the pageant of state.

ii. The English History Play

Argumentative and scholastic drama came with the Reformation; and with the New Learning, as a previous Clark Lecturer observed, came the New Ignorance.[9]

> A levelling, rancorous, rational sort of mind
> That never looked out of the eye of a saint
> Or out of a drunkard's eye.

The moral plays were its product, designed to supplement the Word, and persuade a privileged audience of nobles and clerics. Sermons, not sacraments, gave the model. Many have perished—including a play by the polemical Bale on *The King's Two Marriages*—but more have survived than of the popular drama which is reflected in Spenser's pageants, and which lived only in what Puttenham termed 'the beholding place'.

Ceremony and game prefigured social order. In Caxton's *Game and Play at Chesse* (taken from a French original, and dedicated to George of Clarence) the greater chessmen and the pawns, like the types of Old and New Testaments, linked in pairs, typify the harmonious state of the realm; labourers, smiths, drapers, notaries, taverners, couriers, all given their costumes and attributes, move in their due stations. This game or play of chess or of cards was the subject of several lost interludes; it was revived for the greatest and most scandalous success of the Jacobean stage, Middleton's 'private eye' view of the Prince of Wales's Spanish courtship.

Before the King, Caxton set as his representative the Merchant Pawn; before the Queen, the Physician or Spicer, as her deputy. The relation of 'oppression-protection' between gentry and bourgeois which, according to the Master of Balliol, persisted into the seventeenth century,[10] is represented by conjoining the Knight and the City Porter, the latter

> holding in his right hand great keys and in his left hand a pot and an ell, for to measure with, and ought to have on his girdle a purse open [for toll collections]. And it behoveth that guards and officers of the town be taught and ensigned by the knights that they know and enquire how the city has been governed, which apperteyneth to be kept and defended by the knights.

Here a pageant of civil order stands ready provided. But upset the chessboard and you will be in the midst of a Troublesome Reign, with queens waging war, kings incapable of leadership.

The chief originals of Shakespeare's English history

cycles have long been identified as the clerkly and argumentative Morality plays, even by such acute minds as the late E. M. W. Tillyard, and John Dover Wilson. This view is in need of correction. Shakespeare could not have held the London audience as he did by copying 'morals teaching education'; he and his contemporaries were not, after all, founding a drama, but living in the ruins of a great gild tradition that needed refounding. The Seven Ages of the World became transformed to the Seven Ages of Man, from a solid pageant to an imaginary one—recounted to an exiled duke at a forest meal in Arden. The perspective of acting was achieved by the new Craft Gild of the professional actors and stage poets, concentrating interest on the art of playing—in the modern jargon, on meta-theatre. Microcosm, the world within the heart and body of man, replaced the macrocosmic drama of Total Creation. In the gild plays, shipwrights built the ark; now actors shewed the art of social rôle-taking.

This craft remained collaborative, as was the older craft. Four hands were at work on the Shakespearean *Sir Thomas More*. These plays were fluid as ballads, not yet hardened into literature. We have only to think of the creative instability of such texts as *Richard III*, *Taming of the Shrew* and *Hamlet*. It was the academics that saw tragedy as 'gorgeously embroidered with rich sentences', comedy as 'fair and purfled round with merriments'—yet even here it will be noted, the controlling metaphor is that of a costume.[11]

George Peele, a Londoner born and bred, produced pageants and shews for the City or the Court that were almost pure game; yet their shattered parts, if weaker than the great craft plays, combine ballad material with old Harmony. The suit of glass spangled all over with mirrors which Eleanor of Castile gives to Peele's King Edward I transforms the monarch to something like a mirror for all his subjects, while he remains for the Queen a lover whose image is reflected from her own eyes.

> The welkin spangled through with golden spots
> Reflects no finer in a frosty night

Than lovely Longshanks in his Eleanor's eye,
So Ned thy Nell in every part of thee . . .
Gives glory to those glorious crystal quarries
Where every orb an object entertains
Of rich device and princely majesty
(Scene 3, ll. 704-12)

Elsewhere, however, 'lovely Nell' herself is transformed to a Spanish Fiend, who prescribes mutilation for all her subjects, murders the Lady Mayoress of London, and confesses to treasonous adultery with a friar. This double-visaged Monster (who at one point sinks into the earth as punishment for perjury, to emerge in another part of the City) embodies in a woman's shape the animal nature of a Duessa—a Margaret—a Goneril. These are the devil's miracles, familiar from the feathered and scaly costumes of the old plays.

Monsters, thwarting natural harmony, grow more terrifying when they lack the outward signs of what they are.

Thou changed and self cover'd thing, for shame
Bemonster not thy feature

If a woman's form shield Goneril from her husband's impulse to physical violence, Lear recognizes the fiend that inhabits her as Ingratitude, *more* hideous than the sea monster. And the monsters that teem in Shakespeare's verse—Cowardice, Ignorance, Envy, Jealousy, Conspiracy were physically evoked; they might still be lurking, in plaster or wood, as he picked his way through the property deck. Cowardice has the 'voice of a lion and the acts of a hare'. Elizabeth herself once described such a monster and with her usual prescience termed it a 'hap' or happening.[12] The first recorded reference to Shakespeare the playwright makes just such a monster of him.

This upstart Crow, beautified with our feathers, that with his Tygers heart wrapt in a players hide supposes he is as well able to bombast out a blank verse as the best of you.
(*Greene's Groatsworth of Wit*, 1592)

Beneath a stuffed and plumy costume lurks an ignorant player; and within *his* tough hide, the heart of a ferocious beast. This is no allusion to Horace's Crow or Aesop's Crow, as the learned would have it; Greene is remembering the pageants and 'the sudden appearance of a fabricated Being, made of wood and cloth, entirely invented, corresponding to nothing in Nature'.

The ignorant monster, a sort of Caliban (the monster to end all monsters) tamed and taught language that he turns against his master, belongs, Greene would imply, with the pageants of the old order. Shakespeare for Greene is a species of Caliban.

The break at the Reformation indeed had been traumatic. Social and religious gilds had been suppressed outright; trade gilds saw their pageants censored out of existence. Underlying assumptions and behavioural habits of the audience were however preserved, for it takes several generations to modify these.

The change from one aspect of History to another was not in itself so very difficult; the royal house traced its pedigree back to Seth, and to focus on the English part of the story was only one stage beyond the prefiguration that gave to the figure of King Solomon in King's College Chapel window the face of his descendant King Henry VIII. But a whole area of attendant assumptions and links had been cut by the violence of the Reformation. I have described elsewhere how Marlowe incorporated in *Tamburlaine* icons both of the old and the new faith, effecting a unity beyond logical or argumentative formulation—the Coronation of the Virgin and Foxe's *Acts and Monuments* united as visual symbols.[13] Yet Tamburlaine is also the great iconoclast and by 'leading Fortune tied in a chain' usurps the icon of God himself. Any approach to the white-hot centre of religio-political dispute involved outward risk and inner strain, only to be resolved by paradox. Shakespeare's two plays of religio-political tension stand outside his main cycle, studies in conflict and harmony, confusion and ceremony. The reigns of John and of Henry VIII for sixty years had been linked by moralists as false and true dawn of Reformation; and these constituted the first and last histories he was to write for his own company.

For Shakespeare, in particular, the acceptance of disorder and disintegration made possible a new form. For this most doctrinaire subject was cleared by him of its intransigence. Shakespeare succeeded in treating the virtues of fidelity and patience while defusing the fable of its high explosive charge of religious emnity.

> To arrive at the place where you would be,
> You must go by the place where you are not.

What was necessary for the new genre (Professor Leech has observed)[14] 'was a sense that the action presented had a link with the time in which the play was acted'—it was just, apt, fitting. Instead of forming a great continuum of Seven Ages, Time Past and Time Present were conjoined, as separate identities, by the link between Actor and Audience, also known as separate identities.

The symbolic balance of 'York and Lancaster's long jars' derives from the older cycles; the pattern underlies without dominating the earlier plays, from the destruction of the Garden of England by the deposition of Richard II to the Judgment pronounced on Richard III by the accusing ghosts. The pattern fades in the later plays; the idea of two tetralogies is a bookman's notion, and would scarcely have been accepted by Shakespeare's contemporaries. Nevertheless I am venturing to suggest a new pattern uniting the two non-cycle plays, *King John* and *King Henry VIII*.

Experimental forms were evolved—the Muslim conqueror play, the 'troubles of England'. Shakespeare perhaps modelled *Henry VI* on *Tamburlaine;* but Marlowe had learned from Shakespeare when he wrote *Edward II*. Recognition of these 'kinds' is found in the comments of working dramatists, not theoretically imposed, but identified and transmitted by apprenticeship and practice, as craftsmen everywhere evolve particular styles on which masters of the craft may practise subtle variations.

Endeavour to add unto art, experience [wrote Nashe].
Experience is more profitable void of art than art which hath not
experience. Of itself, art is unprofitable without experience and
experience rash without art.

(*Anatomy of Absurdity*, ed. McKerrow, I, 46.)

As the professional actor drew apart from the audience,
the microcosm that he mimicked in his working drew in
the audience to itself by sympathy. The opening line of
Shakespeare's *Henry VI* 'Hung be the heavens with black,
yield day to night' unites regal and cosmic mourning for
the dead Henry V with the black curtains of the tragic
stage. But the hero Talbot, no image but a living actor,
exploited the responses of the audience till they felt, Nashe
said, that they beheld him fresh bleeding. By their patriot-
ism, the audience, drawn into the play, shed tears for
Talbot.[15] He lived again and died upon the boards, in a
kind of Faustian magic. Followers of the Earl of Shrews-
bury would feel especial warmth as they glanced at the
Talbot on their sleeve; when Oxford, Somerset and
Montague swept in to join the Red Rose of Lancaster,
perhaps the young Earl of Southampton sat in the lords'
room to watch Montague, his maternal ancestor.

Tarlton the Clown linked imagination to revelation and
to satiric wit. Poets search 'the heavens, the earth, the
seas, the shores' that these might serve us a crystal glass,

> To gaze upon our folly
> Wherein our faults are portrayed out,
> Though shews do make us holy.
> (*Tarlton's Tragical Treatises*, 1578)

The frequent stories of guilty creatures sitting at a play,
who, struck to the heart, confessed their malefactions, are
likely to be merely part of the theatre's defence against its
moral opponents, yet they point to the new kind of Transformation which this theatre aimed at, the reaction of one
individual upon another.

Plays were increasingly designed or modified for one
specific occasion or one chief spectator (Peele's *Edward I*
was meant to be part of the post-Armada triumphs in

London). Since the audience no longer consisted of those who had actually built the pageant, they were involved by new techniques of a prologue, a few allusions, a few personal jokes at their expense from the clown, occasionally by topical history of the day, like Marlowe's *Massacre at Paris*.

The early Protestant morality (1536-1543) Bishop Bale's two part pageant of *King Johan* belabours the Papist 'puppetly plays'. In a moral allegory it expounds the story of this 'noble King John' as a faithful Moses that 'withstood Pharaoh for his poor Israel'; which, none the less, remained captive 'Till that duke Josue, which was our late King Henry cleerely brought us in to the land of milk and honey'. In the person of Imperial Majesty, Henry appears at the end of the second part, hangs Sedition, reforms Clergy and instructs both Nobility and Civility; the later version has a prayer for the youthful Queen Elizabeth, designating her as the Angel with the seal. Imperial Majesty denounces Sedition:

> King John ye subdued for that he punished treason,
> Rape, theft and murder in the holy spirituality;
> But Thomas Becket ye exalted without reason
> Because that he died for the Church's wanton liberty.
>
> (ed. Collier, pp. 99-100)

The jesting scurrilities about mixed parties in monasteries, the monkish poisoner who comes to John trolling 'Wassail, wassail' are violently polemical in intent. About the same time, Foxe the Martyrologist also did his best for John as a Morning Star of the Reformation, whilst the early troubles of Queen Elizabeth put her among his sufferers for faith. The Capell collection at Trinity College contains the only surviving copy of a two-part play, which as the Queen's Men are claimed to have acted it in London, should belong to the 1580s. Here John, 'a warlike Christian and your Countryman' is contrasted with the 'Scythian Tamburlaine' by a prologue who offers this dreary play as 'disport'. The audience were apparently prepared to forgo the sword and target fighting if the Papists were sufficiently banged with words. 'Richard Coeur de Lion's base son', advertised on the first title page, is the great innovation; after a court legitimacy trial at which his mother is present, he is asked to give formal testimony, and throws away his inheritance by bursting out of a trance-like silence with some not unfamiliar Latin:

Philippus atavis edite regibus . . .
Quo me rapit tempestas?
What wind of honour blows this fury forth?   (1.1.241-4)

The Total Creation tells him so. However, later in the play, his pretty wit in the familiar game of pillaging monasteries establishes him as a comic character and true forebear of Henry VIII. The sudden death of John, like the abrupt death of Cambises, simply suggests that it is time to stop the play (much as Ralph is exhorted to 'die' in the *Knight of the Burning Pestle*); it is the actor's last 'display'.

Shakespeare adapts the Bastard to the needs of Richard Burbage; this son of the last true king bounds into the family between John the usurper, and Arthur the dispossessed princely heir. A displacement of the Royal image marks the first play on English history which Shakespeare wrote for the great company of the Lord Chamberlain's Men in which he and Burbage were to spend their working lives. It represents the breaking down of some inner rigidity; a kind of subliminal iconoclasm is set within the most doctrinaire of the Protestant histories. Like Richard III and Petruchio, a natural actor, outside the barriers of hierarchy and decorum by his irregular birth, the Bastard Falconbridge as Royal Clown may serve as crystal glass to gaze upon the follies of the times. His irreverent wit and mercurial variety caught in the ruins of the old moral play, shattering its tragic framework. Shakespeare never returned to the tragical history; his later history plays are of a mixed and complex kind that is his own, but to make the transition he went back to a familiar stage story (as later with *Hamlet*). A smooth Italian diplomat replaces the simple scurrilities of the anti-Papal jests, the sophistication of whose technique, though it fails at the end, belongs to the new world of 'observation', a game of chess where everyone courteously plays false:

> 'O sir', says answer 'at your best command;
> At your employment; at your service, sir.'
> 'No, sir' says question, 'I, sweet sir, at yours'
>
> (1.1.197-9)

This is the Bastard, rehearsing in soliloquy the hazards of courtly intercourse. When later he has learnt how far kings will go in treachery to win a royal title, his irony enlarges its scope to a game at bowls with the devil Commodity as opponent, charming the round world to act as his 'wood'.

> Commodity, the bias of the world,
> The world which of itself is poised well,
> Made to run even upon even ground,
> Till this advantage, this vile-drawing bias,
> This sway of motion, this Commodity,
> Makes it take head from all indifferency,
> From all direction, purpose, course, intent.   (2.1.574-80)

As Fortune turns against John, the Bastard, 'lost amid the thorns and dangers of this world' displays a confidence he does not feel and so puts heart into the shattered realm. (The play has always been revived at times of threatened invasion, as in the '45, and during the Napoleonic scares.) By paradox, this irreverent jester upholds, even creates in his valour, whatever national unity survives. He, whose very name had been given away, *is* England (a territorial title usurped and much used by John). With it, he crowns the dead boy Prince Arthur, committing the shattered little body to the arms of Hubert:

> How easily dost thou take all England up!

Shakespeare omits many of the careful logical bridges in the story, established by his predecessor; the narrative itself is wrenched and uncertain.[16] Simple moral certitudes are conspicuous by their absence, in a story which by tradition had for thirty years been filled with them. The very forms of men change with the feelings of beholders; Hubert looks ugly to John as embodying his own fear and remorse, while John to the repentant rebels, looks like an

A CRAFTSMAN'S THEATRE

ocean deity: 'our great King John'. Laments, pleas, tirades, extremes of physical fear, above all, Confusion, are presented in terms of direct sensation, unheroically. Torn between her kinsfolk and her newly plighted husband, a princess cries:

> I am with both, each army hath a hand,
> And in their rage, I having hold of both,
> They whirl asunder and dismember me. (3.1.328-30)

The body of the dead Arthur stupefies:

> Sir Richard, what think you? have you beheld,
> Or have you read or heard? or could you think?
> Or do you almost think, although you see,
> That you do see? could thought, without this object,
> Form such another? (4.3.41-5)

When revenge and rebellion follow, all England, not only warring nobility, is involved. Bewildered under the glare of five moons whirling in the distempered sky, the craftsmen of London panic at news of invasion.

> I saw a smith stand with his hammer thus,
> The while his iron did on his anvil cool,
> With open mouth swallowing a tailor's news;
> Who with his shears and measure in his hand,
> Standing on slippers which his nimble haste
> Had falsely thrust upon contrary feet
> Told of a many thousand warlike French
> That were embattailed and rank'd in Kent.
> (4.2.193-200)

'The giant world enrag'd' drops to the calm of exhaustion after the last struggle, as night comes to part the stumbling weary powers, with the French finally cast away on Goodwin Sands, the English swallowed by Lincolnshire tides.

This is a worldly play, a modern play, its new purpose contemporary social exposure, not obsolete ecclesiastical recrimination. It is post-Reformation but the international threat of war is felt by constituted *nations*, united with the solidity of the sixteenth rather than the thirteenth century.

21

Plays on the troubles of London had been popular throughout the early 1590s; *Henry IV* is centred on London and one of the players' favourite inns, the Boar's Head; yet the northernness of Hotspur, the social relations of Falstaff and the west country worthies witness that Shakespeare knew his country's soil as only actors and soldiers know it—on the soles of his boots.

Henry V, as Hardison noted, is a clear example of ritual form adapted for a secular subject, and, with the flexibility of ritual, it is now presented as an anti-war play. Hal's soliloquy condemning the Idol Ceremony shews how far this play lies from the unambiguous chivalry that still contented some men at the turn of the century.

By this time, the English History had fulfilled its function of relating the old pageants to the new craft of the Player. Although Heywood in Jacobean times still drew crowds to the Red Bull Theatre with the troubles of Queen Elizabeth, citizens beheld themselves in his Plantagenet London in 1599 in a flattering glass. Military discipline and social order prevail, under the Mayor and Sheriffs, when in order of precedence

> Whole companies
> Of mercers, grocers, drapers and the rest
> Are drawn together for their best defence
> Beside the Tower   (*Edward IV*, 1.3)

while their 'prentices shout a challenge from the ranks—cheered no doubt by the modern 'prentices of the pit:

> Nay, scorn us not that we are 'prentices,
> The chronicles of England can report
> The memorable actions we have done.

Meanwhile, Shakespeare turned away to the lives of the noble Romans.

iii. Shakespeare's Epilogue

Let fourteen years pass. In February 1613, London is celebrating the marriage of Elizabeth of Bohemia, while mourning the death of Henry Prince of Wales. The King's

Players put forth the best of their now unequalled craft—pageantry to give the select audience of their expensive theatre the Blackfriars a spectacular triumph, the Game of Chess in all its glory. Playbills might have advertised it:

King Henry VIII or All is True;
shewing the Divorce of Queen Katherine, exactly
as it was seen within this very Great Parliament Chamber
of Blackfriars, as also the Magnificent Coronation of Queen
    Anne,
and the Christening of the Princess Elizabeth,
Heraldry and banners designed and painted by Richard Burbage;
jewels, crowns and Order of nobility exactly copied by Robert
Armin and John Lowin, Goldsmiths and Comedians; the play by
W. Shakespeare, Gent. of Stratford upon Avon, at present
residing in the Gatehouse of Blackfriars.

This was a unique chance to capitalize upon the powerful historic associations of their playhouse, together with an appeal to general patriotic Protestantism.

For Shakespeare had come round to a distinct if somewhat ambiguous treatment of the triumph of Imperial Majesty, the sunrise to which John had been a morning star, the arrival of the Blessed Babe Elizabeth, who is greeted with Messianic prophecy out of Virgil's eclogues. Here, at the end of the play, is the Transformation Scene, the arrival of the wondrous figure who for the audience was a living memory—she had been dead just ten years—but with prophecies that extended to her namesake, the Princess Elizabeth, new wedded to the Protestant Champion and soon to become, briefly, the Winter Queen of Bohemia.

The twinning of King John and King Henry, established by Bale, does not mean that we have a diptych, but there are correspondences between the plays relating them as winter and summer, like the two halves of *The Winter's Tale*. Shakespeare was too profound a craftsman to excogitate his symbolic meanings. The contrast is of Confusion and Harmony, War and Peace, royal weakness and royal supremacy. Henry begins with a triumph over Buckingham, last of the Barons in the old order; the fall of the

Stranger Queen Katherine compares with Constance of Brittany rather than Blanche of Spain; patience is contrasted with impatience. The Church as international power, in both Pandulph and Wolsey threatens the supremacy of the king. At the centre of each play is a Holy Child, the tragic death of Arthur counterpoised by the triumphant birth of Elizabeth. Not the Seven Ages of the World but the Age of Prophecy or of fulfilment provides the time-pattern. *King John* has no tragic shape—it is *'The Life and Death of King John'*; but *The Famous Life of King Henry VIII* carries within it the old tragic image of Fortune's Wheel. The succession of three great figures who fall from power—Buckingham, the Queen, Wolsey, are followed by Cranmer, who speaks a prophecy straight out of Foxe's *Book of Martyrs* as godfather to the Blessed Babe. Few would fail to recollect his terrible and glorious ending in the Town Ditch at Oxford. The Wheel of Fortune is contained within the Sphere of Destiny, and controlled by Providence through Henry, God's chosen vessel.

'Think you behold them living' says the Prologue; Nashe's views on Talbot are still the basis of the dramatic appeal. The processional glories are not merely spectacular (although a later Duke of Buckingham in Charles II's reign would cite 'the great scene in Harry the Eighth' as the pinnacle of shewmanship),[17] for the Coronation of Queen Anne was the triumph of a Londoner. Her father, though ennobled, had been a Citizen and Grocer. Sir Henry Wotton thought the careful reproduction of royal insignia, 'the Knights of the Order with their Georges and Garters, the Guards with their embroidered coats and the like . . . make greatness very familiar if not ridiculous'. The King's Men were *entitled* to wear embroidered coats, of course, and Henry VIII himself, as we have seen, allowed the noble insignia to be reproduced for his theatre at Greenwich; but there, of course, the performance was a private one.

Here, the prologue banteringly reminds the audience that double prices are being charged—seats cost a shilling.

(The epilogue suggests that as the ladies will have been gratified, the disbursing gentlemen must agree with them.) Here is no capping of bawdy verses; no fool; no fights; nothing like the vulgar and unlearned play at the rival house, where at the end of King Henry's reign, Wolsey is still alive and opposing the Lutheran Katherine Parr!

Though Wolsey's part offers great opportunities, this play is designed for the whole company to shew their capacity. It is not a one-man shew, like *King John*. Burbage was willing to share the glory. Wotton called it 'some pieces' of the reign.

In 1628, George Villiers, Duke of Buckingham, who ordered the play to be acted, stayed only till Buckingham was condemned and then left. Within a few weeks he himself fell to an assassin's bullet. Life caught up with art here.

It is said that Shakespeare's instruction to the leading actor came down from Lowin to Davenant, from Davenant to Betterton.[18] In the demonstrations of bluff King Harry's ruggedness, the enthusiasm of the London crowds for pretty faces and royal babies, the roguish gallantries of merry old country lords, the aim was to please by very human contrasts with the grand ceremonial occasions— to add the natural life of Community to the symbolic Hierarchy. Less select audiences were parodied in the crowds that thronged to the Coronation: craftsmen thrust in happy disorder.

> Do you take the court for Paris Garden? you rude slaves, leave
>   your gaping? . . .
> These are the youths that thunder at a playhouse and fight for
>   bitten apples   (5.4.2-3, 65-6)

In spite of its confidence, none of the play is left without a touch of asperity; in the very first scene, Ceremony is both praised and denounced as wasteful excess. Of the victims of Fortune's wheel, Buckingham is one of the old rebellious stock of nobles, Katherine a Spaniard, Wolsey a papal ally. Yet it is Katherine, who is presented with a heavenly crown, in a scene which might have come from a medieval craft cycle, by a troupe of angels with bright gilded vizards; although the spectacular coronation of the London Queen was what Londoners came to see.

If it began at the spring in Blackfriars, by a not inappropriate turn of Fortune's wheel, Shakespeare's Epilogue to his history plays was also the last play to be performed at the old Globe Theatre, where it was transferred for the summer season. On St Peter's Day, 1613, the wadding discharged from a cannon during Wolsey's masque lit upon the thatch, and within an hour the whole of 'that virtuous fabric' was burnt to the ground. A popular ballad describes the spectacle with a detached relish for its scenic possibilities; though reality and danger burst in, the jaunty rhymes suggest that a burning playhouse offered only another kind of spectacle.

> Out run the knights, out run the lords,
> And there was great ado,
> Some lost their hats and some their swords,
> Then out run Burbage too.
>> The reprobates, though drunk on Sunday,
>> Prayed for the fool and Henry Cundy.
>> *O sorrow, pitiful sorrow, and yet all this is true*
>
> The perriwigs and drumheads fry,
> Like to a butter firkin,
> A woeful burning did betide
> To many a good buff jerkin.
>> There with swollen eyes, like drunken Flemings',
>> Distressed stood old stuttering Hemmings.
>> *O sorrow, pitiful sorrow, and yet all this is true*

The playbooks were saved—or a decade later, Henry Condell and John Heminges could not have brought out the folio of Shakespeare's works, with so many plays appearing for the first time. But the Globe Theatre had vanished, and with it many memories.

CHAPTER III

SHAKESPEARE'S GILD OF PLAYERS

i. James Burbage, Founder of the Theatre

THE first of English theatrical dynasties ruled for more than sixty glorious years. James Burbage may claim to have founded the English stage by his building of the first theatre. His son Richard, who created Shakespeare's tragic rôles, created also by the quality of his leadership the uniquely favourable conditions in which Shakespeare, as a member of his company, was able to write. His company was the first to achieve independence and dignity. Cuthbert, Richard's brother, inherited the family position but, being unable to sustain it, ended by losing a portion of his inheritance; he was fortunate that he did not live to see the destruction of his father's playhouse, and his brother's players, by the outbreak of the Civil War.

The story must be reconstructed from legal documents, parish registers and public comment; for the Burbages left no such private papers as those illustrating the fortune of the rival company, directed by the Henslowe-Alleyn family alliance. A picture emerges of a lively energetic race, living a close-knit family life, and in spite of their venturings, fiercely conservative. The Burbages clung to their gains, their old home, their own circle; they did not seek to become country gentry by residence or alliance. They remained shew people; the two quarrels, half a century apart, which mark their entry and exit from the scene, reveal the extent to which acting had prospered under their direction during the intervening years.

In the middle of Queen Elizabeth's reign, actors were playing in the yards (or perhaps the rooms) of London inns, in 'houses, yards, gardens or orchards' and even in the open street. If settled at an inn, they would pay rent, and hire costumes and properties from the 'housekeeper', till they grew deeply in his debt. Though the poorest actors must have been too poor to be trusted, high profits justified high risks and the players must have attracted custom for taproom and ordinary.

Among these players was James Burbage, a joiner by trade, who had taken to acting in hopes to better his luck. In 1572, he headed a players' petition of the leading troupe, Lord Leicester's Men; his son testified that he acted in his youth, but of his skill nothing is known. He allied himself with a moderately wealthy citizen and grocer of Bucklersbury, John Brayne, by marrying his sister Ellen, yet he himself was said not to be worth a hundred marks when by 'earnestly insinuating' in 'sweet and continual persuasions' he extracted a loan from Brayne, and by 'many hundred pounds taken up at interest' launched his venture of building a theatre. The first professional stage buildings in England and the first successful indoor theatre were both erected by James Burbage; it is likely that the joiner himself laboured at the scaffolding as, in the spring of 1576, the structure rose outside the north-east gate of the City, close to Finsbury Fields, on a plot of land which Burbage had leased for twenty-one years. It lay within the jumble of buildings that formed the Liberty of Holywell, in the parish of St Leonard's, Shoreditch; the ground included also an inn, The George, and Burbage himself had a house on Holywell Street, where he could superintend all that went on. He had become a new species of player—a player-housekeeper.

The physical form of the Theatre was not Burbage's invention; its frame was an adaptation of the public playing-place to be found outside the walls of many a town. Within this frame, the players' stage and booth were set up. What Burbage really invented was the Box Office. Strollers playing at a fair or at a market-cross saw crowds swiftly melt before the shaken money box; innkeepers fleeced their tenants, driving them to pledge and forfeit their poor stock. In spite of his financial troubles, Burbage from the first enjoyed success; he could station gatherers at the entrance to collect their penny (which went to the players) and another set of gatherers at the scaffolding, to collect another penny (which went to the housekeeper), with further sums for special seats. The commercial and social consequences of the building were to become much more influential than the form of the building itself.

In a twelvemonth's time, another theatre, the Curtain, had sprung up in Holywell and within a few years it was taken over by Burbage for use as an overflow house.

The Theatre was worth quarrelling about. James was still in debt, and extorted more from Brayne. At a scrivener's he struck Brayne with his fist and both 'went together by the ears'. In 1579 he was arrested for debt when on the way to play at the Cross Keys Inn, his company's winter quarters. The legal war, begun by his brother-in-law and extended by his ground landlord Giles Allen—no relation of Alleyn the player—led to suits and cross-suits in the Queen's Bench and Star Chamber, which pestered James Burbage from 1585, and were not settled till 1602, five years after his death.

They were marked by bitterness and cunning, as well as occasional violence. At the present day, Burbage would have become an expert in manipulation of expense accounts and income tax evasion. As it was, he mortgaged his property, and had it redeemed by his elder son Cuthbert, in whose name it then stood.

In 1590, when Mrs Brayne (now a widow) brought some helpers and attempted as a 'sharer' to take up gatherings at the Theatre, James Burbage and his wife, leaning out of a window, called them thieves and whores. Cuthbert came to reinforce the vocal exchange, but the leading rôle was played by sixteen-year-old Richard, who stood

> with a broom staff in his hand, of whom when this deponent asked what stir was there, he answered in laughing phrase how they come for their moiety. But quoth he (holding up the broom staff) I think I have delivered them a moiety with this, and sent them packing.

One of Mrs Brayne's party testified that

> the said Richard Burbage, scornfully and disdainfully playing with this deponent's nose, said that if he dealt in this matter, he

29

would beat him also; and did challenge the field of him at this time.[1]

On several occasions James Burbage was summoned before the magistrates for permitting 'unlawful assemblies' at his Theatre. Malice alleged that he used a false key to rob the collecting box, and that when takings were shared 'he would thrust some of the money devident between himself and his fellows in his bosom or otherwise about his body'. He quarrelled with the Admiral's Men, who left his Theatre for Henslowe's. But there is no real evidence that he treated his fellow players as badly as he treated his brother-in-law. By 1584, when he was summoned by the Lord Mayor to hear an inhibition of plays, the 'stubborn fellow' sent word that 'he was my Lord of Hunsdon's man and that he would not come at me, but that he would in the morning ride to my lord'. He had therefore transferred from Leicester's service to that of Baron Hunsdon, and he provides the link between the first great Elizabethan company, Leicester's Men, and the second great company, which was formed in 1594, when the theatres reopened after a long and hard season of plague.

ii. Shakespeare's Choice

Shakespeare at the age of thirty joined this company; and remained with it for the rest of his working life. He was already well known as a playwright and poet, in 1592, when plague closed the theatres for two years. Others testified that he had the 'gentle' manners of fine breeding, and was 'civil' in demeanour; he was called 'friendly' Shakespeare. Years later, John Davis of Hereford wrote 'To our English Terence, Mr Will. Shakespeare':

> Some say, good Will, which I in sport do sing,
> Had thou not played some kingly parts in sport,
> Thou hadst been a companion for a king,
> And lived a king among the meaner sort.

> (*Scourge of Folly*, 1611, p. 76)

A Wheel of Fortune, *Memento Mori*, and Tree of Life

(*A Fifteenth-century woodcut*)

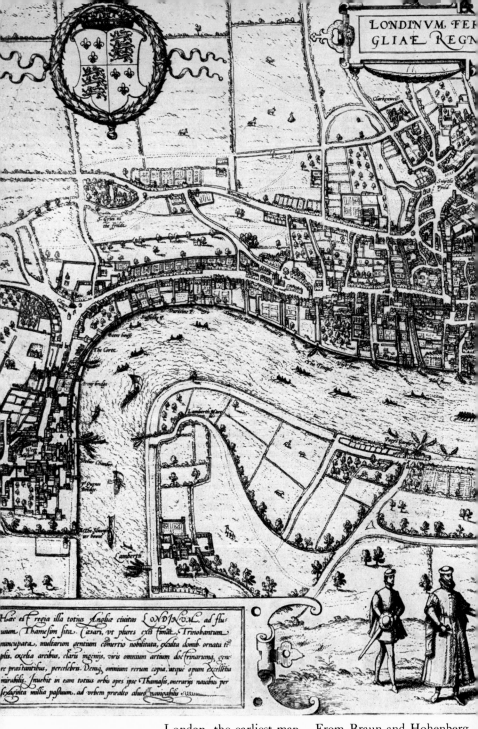

London, the earliest map. From Braun and Hohenberg,

By courtesy of the

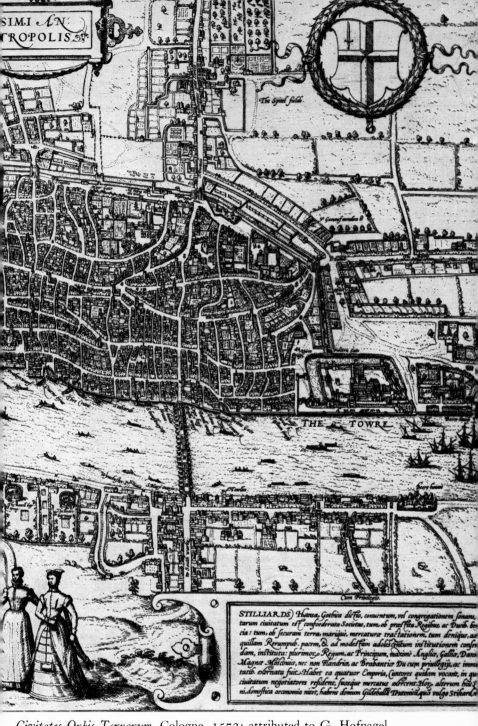

Civitates Orbis Terrarum, Cologne, 1572; attributed to G. Hofnagel.

Edward VI is at the top of Fortune's Wheel, and rising on the wheel, to the right, are Somerset, Archbishop Cranmer and the Council. The dying Henry VIII sinks as he points to his heir, and the Pope is at the bottom of the wheel.

Had Shakespeare ever tried the personally based life of courtly patronage and place seeking, the traditional and nobler one for the poet? Spenser had done so and knew from experience 'what hell it is in suing long to bide'; so did John Lyly. During the plague years Shakespeare may well have retreated to some country house, as did Marlowe and Nashe. Early in 1593 he published his 'diploma piece', his challenge for courtly poetic stakes, *Venus and Adonis*, dedicated to the Earl of Southampton. From this elegant poem he derived a reputation that soon made the undergraduates of Cambridge speak very respectfully of him, even while they sneered at the plays he wrote.

Shakespeare's work, inevitably, is not all extant. *Troilus and Cressida* was printed as an afterthought, *Pericles* appeared much later, *Cardenio* and *Love's Labour's Won* perished. In the *Sonnets* he may be seen taking part in a poetry competition before his patron. (These too, were printed, it would seem, without the author's knowledge.) The twin sonnets, 85 and 86, describe a contest in praise of his lord; the winning verses, in the traditional manner, were to be 'reserved in characters with golden quill'. To explain this line—which no one has done so far—we should look at the Great Festival of the Pui, the foreign merchants of London, a gild dating from Chaucer's day.

After the gild had elected its annual Prince, poets competed with songs of praise, 'and the old Prince and the new Prince ought to decide as to the songs, with those of the companions that understand it best, to the number of fifteen at the most'. The winning song, plainly and correctly set down, was hung up under the Prince's arms, after it had been performed by singers seated on cloth of gold. The winner was then given a 'crown' and rode through the City between the old and the new Princes.[2]

Evidence that such games persisted in Tudor times include the challenge to Edward Alleyn to engage in a contest for the actor's crown.[3] From these sonnets it seems that the rival poet, beginning grandly, so visibly delighted his patron as to fill Shakespeare with alarm. When his turn came, he 'dried'—the actor's worst fear, described in Sonnet 23. He protests, however, that it is no magic spell which has so petrified or 'astonished' him, but fear of losing the real prize—his patron's love and favour.

Sonnet 85

My tongue tied Muse in manners holds her still,
While comments of your praise, richly compiled,
Reserve their character with golden quill
And precious phrase by all the Muses filed.
I think good thoughts, while others write good words,
And, like unlettered clerk, still cry 'Amen'
To every hymn that able spirit affords
In polished form of well refined pen.
Hearing you praised, I say, ' 'Tis so, 'Tis true',
And to the most of praise add something more;
But that is in my thought, whose love to you,
Though words come hindmost, holds his rank before.
    Then others for the breath of words respect,
    Me for my dumb thoughts, speaking in effect.

Sonnet 86

Was it the proud full sail of his great verse,
Bound for the prize of all too precious you,
That did my ripe thoughts in my brain inhearse,
Making their tomb the womb wherein they grew?
Was it his spirit, by spirits taught to write
Above a mortal pitch, that struck me dead?
No, neither he, nor his compeers by night,
Giving him aid, my verse astonished.
He, nor that affable familiar ghost
Which nightly gulls him with intelligence,
As victors of my silence cannot boast;
I was not sick of any fears from thence:
    But when your countenance filled up his line,
    Then lacked I matter; that enfeebled mine.

The kind of retreat which the poet may have enjoyed is depicted in the little academe of *Love's Labour's Lost*— a life of ceremony where anyone might find himself suddenly taking a dramatic rôle, becoming a Russian in compliment to a Princess who had travelled the length of France, or inadequately playing the Nine Worthies. The number of women's parts in this play suggests that it was not written for an ordinary troupe, as do the quantity of private jests. Two years after the most courtly poet since Chaucer had thrown in his lot with blood and slapstick, his whole company went down at Christmas to the Earl of Rutland's country seat, where their performance alternated with that of the household—a noble masquerade was followed, in the way of Christmas cheer, by *Titus Andronicus*!

If this may not have been a willing choice, it was undoubtedly a wise one.

> Oh, for my sake do you with Fortune chide,
> The guilty goddess of my harmful deeds,
> That did not better for my life provide
> Than public means, which public manners breeds.
> Thence comes it that my name receives a brand,
> And almost thence my nature is subdued
> To what it works in, like the dyer's hand . . .
>
> (Sonnet 111)

Forty years ago, T. W. Baldwin compared the players' companies to gilds, the sharers to masters and the hired men to journeymen.[4] The analogy is not exact, for play sharers contracted a joint financial responsibility like that of a modern trading company. In this incorporation of Idleness, the hired men had no rights; this was individualism, 'City doctrine' as Dekker called it. In a study of 'The Livery Companies of Tudor London' (*History*, vol. 61, 1966), T. F. Reddaway suggests that craft production was giving way to merchant venturing, and Christopher Hill has recently reminded us that

> we should not be sentimental about the gilds in our period, whatever they had been earlier. They were usually controlled by oligarchy and were often employers' rings.
> (*Reformation to Industrial Revolution*, 1967, p. 71)

The players' troupes derived from very ancient traditions of personal service to a lord, but their financial methods belonged to the new era. They offer a most striking example of how a new enterprise could be established in response to the quite special demands of the capital city.

In one matter Shakespeare was highly individual. He did not bring his family to London, but lodged first in St Helen's, Bishopsgate (where he was behindhand with his rates); then on the South Bank among rival groups of actors; later he moved back to Cripplegate on the north side of the City and lodged with a Huguenot family. But in 1596, through his father, he applied for a coat of arms; the next year he bought New Place at Stratford, near the beautiful gild chapel which, with the house, had been built by Sir Hugh Clopton, Lord Mayor of London. Shakespeare kept up with his Stratford friends—a Stratford man had printed *Venus and Adonis*—advancing small loans, attending to their business in town. At home in vacation, like any other city magnate with a country seat, he could have lived in leisure among his gentlemanly friends, buying up tithes, sleeping in his orchard of an afternoon. He made friends with the Russells and Digges, minor gentry, and eventually married his elder daughter to a sound professional man, with a Cambridge degree, and a medical practice among the nobility.

Life in country society carried more true gentility than the dangerous scramble for court favours, and compensated for the social insecurity of the stage. Shakespeare succeeded naturally in living two separate kinds of life, each selected with a firm sense of its adjustment to the other. This in itself was something of a social feat at a time when most people had a single environment and expected to stay there, without making adjustments, still less being all things to all men.[5]

But if his social life varied, his professional duty was unwavering. At the beginning of the 1590s, there were still all kinds of entertainments at the theatre, and the life of the different troupes was fluid and shifting. By the end of the 1590s, the theatre had settled down, and by the end of the next decade, had taken its modern form. In the 1580s four men and a boy made up a troupe; but eight became usual a decade later. Fifteen actors appeared in

Julius Caesar in 1599, including of course the hired men. By Charles I's reign over thirty men were enrolled among the King's Men.

John Davies of Hereford, in the poem already quoted, implies that Shakespeare's reputation assisted his company:

> Some others rail; but rail as they think fit,
> Thou hast no railing but a reigning wit:
> And honesty thou sowest, which they do reap,
> So to increase their stock, which they do keep.

That sounds rather like a hit at James Burbage. But for Shakespeare doubtless the important connection was with Richard, who had already probably played some of his parts, but for whom Shakespeare was to devise Romeo and Mercutio's wit combats, the Bastard, and eventually his greatest tragedies. A contemporary wit among the lawyers recorded a piece of folklore about the two[6]:

> Upon a time when Burbage played Richard III, there was a Citizen grew so far in love with him that before she went from the playhouse she sent for him to come unto her that night by the name of Richard III. Shakespeare overhearing their conclusion went before, was entertained and at his game ere Burbage came. Then message being brought that Richard III was at the door, Shakespeare caused answer to be made that William the Conqueror came before Richard III.
>
> (*Manningham's Diary*, 13 March 1661/2)

The development of acting is notoriously difficult to estimate; a generation earlier it is clear that there could have been little co-ordination. Puttenham spoke of 'poets that wrote only for the stage . . . plays and interludes for recreation' to 'set forth in shews and pageants accompanied with speech the common behaviours and manners of private persons'—almost a dumb shew with Presenter. At the point where the history play was beginning to emerge, in 1565, Apius the unjust judge of *Apius and Virginia* exclaims:

> But out! I am wounded; how I am divided,
> The states of my life soon from me are glided.

The following remarkable stage direction ensues: 'Here let him make as though he went out and let Conscience and Justice come out of him, and let Conscience have in his hand a burning lamp, and let Justice have a sword and hold it before Apius.' These two, after speaking of themselves as members of the judge—they are live actors, not puppets—take their leave. It must be assumed that they crept out from his skirts, as he stood by the door. The regular doubling of parts in a significant way, as when in Bale's *King Johan* one actor may play Usurped Power and the Pope, culminated in monodramas where a single actor took *all* the parts. As late as the seventeenth century, household fools would provide this kind of entertainment. In *Euphues* it is said 'He that always playeth one part bringeth loathsomeness to the ear. It is variety that moveth the mind of all men'.

But with the growth of dramatic companies, Protean variety within the single parts, or contrast of one part with another emerged. Acting as a craft depended on the ensemble, and so, it may be hazarded, did play-writing. The plays written for the rival house, Alleyn's and Henslowe's, remained shapeless. Though Mundy, its 'best plotter', outlined stock rôles crudely and firmly, yet among the simpler artisans, if any continued, Snug the joiner must still assure his royal auditory that he is not a lion. Burbage enjoyed lines of sardonic wit; instead of doubling rôles, he preferred a single character, which in itself united contradictory and paradoxical elements. His well-known 'Protean' temperament meant 'that he never put off his part, no, not so much as in the tiring house till he had finished, still with looks and gestures maintaining it to the heighth'[7] so, he could interpret complex rôles, culminating of course in Hamlet.

The Theatre itself provided a conditioning social structure; not only reproducing but creating the social dynamic of the actor-audience relation. The grades of seating, the relation of one part of the audience to the rest also imposes a social relation which moulds the total dramatic response. Those seated on the stage had a natural incentive to act—

they were the Chief Spectators or Lords in whose honour all was done. When in 1564, Queen Elizabeth saw a play in King's College Chapel, a great platform was built in front of the screen, where she sat on the south side, visible to all, while the actors, using side-chapels as tiring houses, played on the north side. Both would be in profile to the audience, seated in the ante chapel. Elsewhere, chief spectator and actors shared the floor, with spectators crowded in galleries above.

In 1596, turned out of the Inns that were their winter quarters by the City Fathers, the Burbages sought to acquire a distinguished Hall Theatre by purchase for £600 of the Great Parliament Chamber at Blackfriars. Its associations were noble—too noble—for the Lord Chamberlain and other inhabitants of the building forbade its use for plays as disturbing to their privacy.

At private theatres, Chief Spectators sat on the stage, but not at the people's playhouse. At the centre of Burbage's stage, stood a Man—the masterpiece of the Supreme Craftsman, and how unlike an image. For Hamlet the sky has become only a canopy over a stage, Denmark a jutting promontory; but when he thinks of the actor—

> What a piece [that is a masterpiece] of work is a man! how noble in reason, how infinite in faculties, in form and moving; how express and admirable in action, how like an Angel, how like a God! (2.2.323-7)

The Quarto punctuation gives you the picture of a performance in a rather old-fashioned gild play.

The greatest Castle Hall in Northern Europe, at Elsinore, has no galleries; but it was hung with tapestries representing the former Kings of Denmark—ideal for comparing one king with another, or for concealment. The chequered marble floor could have been paced off for duels. This scene of course was unknown to the audience but English actors had been to Elsinore. For the rest the audience were likely to interpret any scene in local terms, as they had done since the miracle plays.

The County Paris, at St Peter's Church,
Shall happily make thee there a joyful bride.

(3.5.115-6)

says Lady Capulet to Juliet. For a Londoner this meant the Collegiate Church of St Peter at Westminster. If Juliet had an Abbey wedding why not an Abbey funeral? Perhaps the Abbey tombs provide the answer to the long-disputed crux of how Juliet's tomb was staged. At the Abbey it is necessary to ascend to the royal monuments; could her tomb have been on the *upper* stage, tragically identified with the bed chamber, and reached by the same external stairs, at the top of which Romeo forces the door? I tender this suggestion to the next producer in search of a novelty.

In February 1597, in his sixty-seventh year, James Burbage died and his coffin was borne to the parish church of St Leonard's whither the coffins of so many little Janes, Juliets and Alices of his family had preceded him, in grim witness to the insalubrious nature of Shoreditch. Six months later the burial of an infant James, son of Cuthbert Burbage, was recorded. In all six children of Richard and two of Cuthbert died in infancy. Of Shakespeare's three, in the healthier climate of Stratford, two survived.

Still harassed by lawsuits, James had mortgaged the Theatre, and had it redeemed by his elder son Cuthbert in whose name it then stood; to Richard the sharp-witted old snatcher had bequeathed his unused playhouse at Blackfriars and the leadership of the acting troupes.

iii. Shews at the Globe

So, under the youthful leadership of their star, the company entered on a period of greatest splendour. Richard Burbage gained their full co-operation by sharing his inheritance with them. Troubles with their ground landlord continued, as the lease of the Theatre was about to expire. The company extricated themselves by applying the old troupers' mobility to their new fixed asset. On the day after Christmas Day, 1598, they assembled at night, armed and accompanied by twelve workmen, dismantled the entire wooden structure of the interior of the Theatre, took it across the river and there erected it to form the seating of their new house, The Globe, on a site secured by a thirty-one-year lease. The landlord was left with the forlorn shell of an empty ring and the chance to sue them for trespass; the players were left with the little Curtain Theatre (close by) as their only home. The joiners' marks on the wood, which perhaps James Burbage had cut himself, would have enabled them to refit the structure together plank for plank.[8] It is not known of course whether Shakespeare actually helped shiver the timbers. By the spring of 1599 all was ready, and Peter Street their carpenter was busy on a new theatre for their rivals. Shakespeare as a Southwark resident was specially noted by the new ground landlord, Nicholas Brend, when on 16 May, 1599, the inventory of his goods listed 'une doma de nove edificata ... in occupatione Guillielme Shakespeare et aliorum'.

To finance the Globe Theatre, the Burbage brothers had parted with a moiety. This moiety was shared between five players, including Shakespeare. So that he was now a part-owner of the playhouse, as well as a sharer in the company of players.

The playhouse was a sign of the company's prosperity and good standing. It was mentioned in the Letters Patent by which James I licensed them as his own, with right to perform 'within their now usual playhouse, The Globe, within our county of Surrey' or elsewhere. He also gave them scarlet cloth for liveries and they marched at the Coronation.

As a fellowship of players, the group had been responsible for paying the hired men, for costumes, lighting and properties. Now they were also responsible for the upkeep of the fabric, and shared in all the takings. Richard had shared where his father had snatched. The Burbages remained in their old house in Holywell, where an actors' colony had grown up. Like other craftsmen, actors lived in the same neighbourhood, intermarried, stood sponsors to each other's children and remembered one another in their wills.

Perhaps because he had to borrow more money at interest, Richard Burbage let his private playhouse in Blackfriars to the syndicate that controlled the children of the Chapel Royal, sometime late in the autumn of 1600. (Their private playing could not be stopped.) The result was surprising; a new, peppery and spicy brand of acting upset the authorities and started up the Theatre War. 'How are they escoted?'—or 'Who pays the rent?' asked their goaded landlord in his character of Hamlet Prince of Denmark.

Different kinds of audience were emerging—that was the lesson of the little boys' success. Musical concerts replaced clowning for the entr'actes. Was it possible in one theatre to appeal to very different expectations, to evoke something for an audience that was becoming individualized in its demands?

The answer is found in the 'great decade' of the English theatre, and Shakespeare's series of tragic masterpieces, *Hamlet*, *Macbeth*, *Lear*, *Othello*. James Burbage had built a theatre; Shakespeare and Richard built in human materials. The growing range and power of Shakespeare's verse bears witness to the growing range and flexibility of the actors. Burbage was reputed a good trainer of youth and took apprentices; a contemporary play shews him giving an audition, the acknowledged lord of the London stage.

Burbage also had some talent as a painter, and it may be that many of the actors pursued other crafts as sidelines, for their wills often describe them as tradesmen of the City. Shakespeare and Burbage once shared the designing of a tilting shield for the Earl of Rutland.

Shakespeare was master of many styles—*Troilus and Cressida*, for instance, was perhaps specially oriented, though the cost of mounting, rehearsing and putting on a play meant that even the greatest did not commission special productions, only special performances.

A growing sense of the history of their craft is attested by the Jacobean players' burlesques of older forms. The old Hamlet, the old Jeronimo or Hotspur, favourite part of Ralph the Grocer's 'prentice in *The Knight of the Burning Pestle,* were recalled as we might recall early Noël Coward. Ralph's mistress, who does not know how to behave in a 'modern' playhouse, and who has never seen anything but fairground shews, is a jest for seasoned playgoers, like the fatuous young man depicted by Dekker in *The Gull's Hornbook.* The playwrights now feel sure enough of the different 'kinds' to mock them or pretend not to conform. We have heard Shakespeare in the prologue to *Henry VIII* assuring the audience this is not the usual history. It took Heywood another twelve years before he could boast that his play (*The English Traveller*) had neither drum, trumpet, dumb shew, combat, marriage, song or dance; ten years later still, Shirley was apologising for offering no fights, shews, dances, bawdry, ballads, clowns, squibs, or devils.

The modern theatre effectually began when Burbage regained possession of the Blackfriars in the autumn of 1608. Sharing was on a more generous scale than before; all the company held alike in the new house. An indoor stage brought new techniques; yet Shakespeare paradoxically recalls and transforms the romances of his youth, as the links with the old craft stage disappeared.[9] As the Globe was still popular, actors had to be very adaptable. *Henry VIII* began expensively at Blackfriars and moved to the popular theatre in the summer. After the burning of the Globe, the actors within a year raised the money to rebuild it, on the old plan; it cost fourteen hundred pounds, a sum which only a wealthy group could have provided, representing the equivalent of a year's revenue. In 1600 the Fortune Theatre had been built at a third of the cost.

Soon after, in 1616, Shakespeare died at Stratford, leaving a remembrance each to Burbage, Heminges and Condell. A son born to Richard soon afterwards was baptised William; he was the only male Burbage of the third generation to reach maturity.

Three years later, still at the height of his powers—

though Field was now in the juvenile lead—Richard
Burbage was smitten with a paralytic stroke. His brother
Cuthbert drew up his will; he died and was buried in St
Leonard's, 16 March, 1619, at the age of forty-five. He
was said to have died with more than £300 a year in land,
a fortune on a par with Shakespeare's but far below that
of Edward Alleyn.

A stream of elegies and tributes followed; the Earl of
Pembroke in a private letter declared he had no heart to
attend the play 'so soon after the death of my old acquain-
tance Burbage'. There was not a dry eye in London, for
'Dick Burbage was their mortal god on earth'. In spite of
youthful rivals, he remained 'the Actor's clearest light, in
no dark time'.

iv. The Later History

Perhaps it was his death which led Heminges and
Condell to publish Shakespeare's works, which while he
lived seemed but cold immortality to what his acting could
bestow. Lowin and Taylor took over the leads, while
Heminges was the business head of the company. Burbage's apprentice went to live with Cuthbert; something
of the fellowship remained. The will of this apprentice,
drawn in 1623, left his estate to Heminges and Cuthbert,
gratefully recalled the kindness of Cuthbert's wife Elizabeth, who witnessed with her mark, and remembered also
Mrs Condell, Richard's small daughter, and his sister.
But with Burbage's death the family claims dwindled to
those of capitalists. After a second prolonged closure for
plague, at the time of King James's death, the King's Men
emerged as the only stable company, Alleyn's company
being ruined by a disastrous fire in 1621, when their plays
were lost. The history of Caroline drama centres on this
group. Control became increasingly exerted by a shrinking
group of older men, and after the death of Heminges in
1630, there was a revolt. The Blackfriars was by now
popular enough to cause in 1633 the first recorded traffic
jam in London. Thirty-five men were covered by the

Company's Letters Patent. Three of them sought a more equal distribution of the shares, and they appealed to the Lord Chamberlain, Herbert, who upheld them. Members of the craft gilds were forbidden to go to law; differences must be settled in the gild. Customary ties prevailed over legal rights, they did not seek the justice of the courts.[10] The case went to arbitration finally, and the outcome is unknown.

Vainly old Cuthbert Burbage pleaded the long story of his family's early struggle, against 'these new men so soon shot up . . . that were never bred from children in the king's service' (one had been an actor ten years!).

Though out of Richard Burbage's estate so many other actors had been maintained, his brother had to learn the lesson James had taught John Brayne—there was no room in shew business for sleeping partners. An old clown who also held many shares pleaded that he trained boys, but found himself barred from the stage. The shock and distress may have proved fatal to both, for John Shanks died in January, 1636, and Cuthbert Burbage the following October, in his father's old house in Holywell. Richard's son William went off to Barbados, and so ended the dynasty of the Burbages.

The King's Men became the most successful troupe because it represented a co-partnership. 'He incorporates himself under title of a brotherhood' was said of a player as late as 1615; legal incorporation might be achieved by the players entering into a 'merry bond' for a fictitious debt. It appears that the hired men were paid by verbal agreement; if takings were poor they would not receive full wages. But the capital outlay connected with stock and buildings, and the tighter legal obligations connected with the ownership of property, required an arrangement more precise than the sharing of daily takings. New forms of trade affected the stage. One of the problems was the widows' jointures, which frequently led to disputes; one led to a Chancery suit, destroying the company at the Red Bull; Heminges's daughter also sued her own father on this issue.[11] By 1635, the struggle in the King's Men had almost become one between Equity and Management. In other companies, the financiers exploited their actors with impunity, as in Beeston's notorious Young Company. Beeston represented himself as 'Governor' of a troupe of boys, when most of them were not boys at all.

Old forms and old traditions persisted, while new habits grew up; although the new men could be ruthless in pursuit of their rights, plays and acting remained in the accepted patterns which they had been given by Shakespeare and his generation. This may be illustrated from one of the latest of the Caroline working-playwrights, Dick Brome. He began life as the personal servant of Ben Jonson, and worked back-stage, but his plays also shew deeply the influence of Shakespeare, and in particular those precepts to the actors set out in *Hamlet*. Not only Jonson but Dekker, Jonson's old enemy, called Dick Brome 'son'; and noble amateurs, such as Thomas Stanley, commended him. Brome's comedies look forward to the Restoration, yet he gives us glimpses into a tiring-house on two levels which suggests that the players still hoarded their old property monsters. In *The Antipodes*, a mad young man, who is shewn a comedy to cure his disordered wits and bring him to more ordinary modes of behaviour, invades first the property deck on the ground floor, then the wardrobe, housed at gallery level.

> 'has got into our tiring-house among us,
> And ta'en a strict survey of all our properties,
> Our statues and our images of gods; our planets and our constellations,
> Our giants, monsters, furies, beasts and bugbears,
> Our helmets, shields and vizors, hairs and beards,
> Our pasteboard marchpane, and our wooden pies,

Brandishing a sword, which luckily is 'no blade, but a rich scabbard with a lathe in't' he

> rusheth among the foresaid properties,
> Kills monster after monster, takes the puppets
> Prisoners, knocks down the cyclops, tumbles all
> Our jigembobs and trinckets to the wall.

44

Spying at last the crown and royal robes
I' the upper wardrobe, next to which by chance
The devils' vizors hung, and their flame-painted
Skin coats, those he removed with greater fury
And (having cut the infernal ugly faces
All into mammocks) with a reverend hand
He takes the imperial diadem and crowns
Himself the King of the Antipodes.
(*The Antipodes*, 1640, ed.
Ann Haaker, 1966, 3.6.3-8, 19-30)

Here is the old Elizabethan theatre, presided over by
old Lord Letoy—for these are his household players,
whom he maintains in princely style: he himself dresses
plainly but they look like an emperor's men, and he recalls
the style of the 'English Earl' that had 'once so loved a
play and players'—Leicester, original founder of the
troupe. He boasts

These lads can act the Emperors' lives all over,
And Shakespeare's chronicled histories to boot.
(1.5.66-7)

and not only writes plays for them, but instructs them, in
a fashion which shews how completely Shakespeare had
defined their own function for the actors.

Let me not see ye act now
In your scholastic way you brought to town wi' ye,
With a see-saw sack-a-down, like a sawyer;
Nor in a comic scene play *Hercules Furens*,
Tearing your throat to split the audient's ears.
And you, sir, you had got a trick of late
Of holding out your bum in a set speech,
Your fingers fibulating on your breast,
As if your buttons or your band-strings were
Helps to your memory . . .   (2.1.16-25)

The reproaches include 'overacting of the legs' like a dancing master, and pirouettes:

And when you have spoke, at end of every speech,
Not minding the reply, you turn you round,

45

SHAKESPEARE THE CRAFTSMAN

As tumblers do, when between every feat
They gather wind by firking up their breeches.

(2.1.30-2)

Brome himself was a modest author, who did not, like
Jonson, threaten the actors' lives if they changed the
speeches. James Shirley, a Cambridge graduate, praised
him for his practical training:

Learning, the file of poesy, may be
Fetcht from the arts and universitie;
But he that writes a play and good, must know
Beyond his books, men and their actions too.

Here was a revolution from the day half a century earlier
when Robert Greene, Master of Arts, had considered it
presumption for Shakespeare to take to the art of play-
writing!

In *The Antipodes*, the world of London is shewn 'upside
down'—a country where old men go to school, old women
are restrained by their grand-daughters from frequenting
plays and bear-baiting. This upside-down vision which
cures the mad young man depends on the Londoners'
long familiarity with scenes of their own society. The play
provides a new mirror both for players and for audience.
Brome, the good craftsman, recognized most fully the kind
of transformation which Shakespeare and Jonson had
brought about together, setting the world of the play
against the world of ordinary life. This replaced the older
configurations of medieval times, yet evoked similar depth
and involvement to the performance, although its basis
was different. The actors are given status and their social
identity recognized when they are reflected *within* the play.

The play scenes in *Hamlet* may now appear merely
episodic; but it is not accident that they form part of the
first great tragedy of the modern stage. This moment of
recognition, though apparently only of technical interest,
is a symbol of deep security and confidence. It accompanies,
like a catalyst, the more profound re-orientations of plot
and character.

Dick Brome, in *The Jovial Crew* (1652), also wrote the

46

Epilogue to the whole glorious history.[12] For this play
'had the luck to tumble last of all in the Epidemical ruin
of the scene' and, being the latest play performed before
the theatres were closed, it mirrors the lot of the actors,
when even the best were being turned out to the beggary
that long had stigmatized masterless men. With one excep-
tion, all the King's players gave or hazarded their lives in
the war for their master.

Facing this tragic collapse, Brome wrote neither a
tragedy nor a satire, but a gay little comedy. The gallantry
of spirit that rises when things grow black made him
identify masters and men. In a springtime frolic, a quartet
of young lovers, country gentlefolks, set off to masquerade
as beggars and end as strolling actors, performing their
own story as a play. It is the converse of Sly's adventure in
The Taming of the Shrew. A 'precise' young steward joins
the frolic and introduces his young mistresses and their
gallants to a crew of beggars and to their cant—these are
'the jovial crew' or 'the merry beggars'. As Brome says in
his introduction 'If the time make us beggars, let us make
ourselves merry'.

The lovers are commended for their resolution

> t'expose yourselves,
> Brave volunteers, unpress'd by common need,
> Into this meritorious warfare
> (ed. Ann Haaker, 1968, 2.1.327-9)

while the ladies long for the free state of a beggar's life:

> to feast and revel, here today and yonder tomorrow; next day
> where they please; and so on still, the whole country or kingdom
> over. There's liberty—the birds of the air can take no more.
> (2.1.19-22)

They quickly learn the real hardship of living like beggars,
and their own ineptitude at the beggars' trade provides the
comedy. Youthful spirits, the aristocratic wilfulness of the
frolic is given a deeper note by the wisdom of the steward,
their servant:

> They know (and so may you) this is your birthright into a new
> world. And we all know (or have been told) that all come crying

into the world, when the whole world of pleasures is before us.
The world itself had ne'er been so glorious, had it not first been
a confus'd chaos. (3.1. 33-8)

From such a confused chaos the players had built their
'second world' of art; as they saw violence rise all round,
they made their final bow in a gay little comedy, trans-
posing the world of Florizel and Perdita into that of a
harsher reality with defiant grace. Brome's final act of
craftsmanship justifies the praise of his old master, Jonson:

> I had you for a servant, once, Dick Brome;
> And you perform'd a servant's faithful parts:
> Now, you are got into a nearer room
> Of Fellowship, professing my old arts. . . .
> You learn't it well and for it serv'd your time,
> A prenticeship; which few do nowadays. . . .
> It was not so of old; men took up trades
> That knew the crafts they had been bred in right,
> An honest bilbo smith would make good blades. . . .
>
> (Verses prefixed to *The Northern Lass*, 1632)

The blades were drawn now in earnest; the games of
ceremony at Whitehall and on the common stages alike
had ended. There remained only the last tragic scaffold,
awaiting its Royal Actor

> While round the armed bands
> Did clap their bloody hands.

CHAPTER IV

THE NEW CLOWN: TWELFTH NIGHT

i. Robert Armin

PERHAPS the most difficult problem for Shakespeare the dramatist was the control of the clown. 'In the days of Tarlton and of Kempe' clowns not only ad-libbed; they would 'kill' a scene by holding, as Brome testified, 'interlocutions with the audience'.[1] Very early popular merriments were largely mock-fights; such bantering from the courtly audience as Shakespeare evidently knew himself, to judge from *Love's Labour's Lost*, established a relationship highly provocative, not easily controlled. At the end of a public play came the clown's 'jig' or an improvised game of rhyming with the crowd. Clowns wrote their own plays—Tarlton's *Seven Deadly Sins* was successful; Kempe's *Knack to Know a Knave* is a robust merriment of the Wise Fools of Gotham. The unity of dramatic ensemble was completed only when the fool became absorbed in the group relations of the play itself.

The old level of exchange is suggested by a rhyme contest between Henry VIII and his jester Will Summers, which comes to conclude one of Rowley's plays. The Emperor is judge.

KING. Answer this, sir. 'The bud is spread, the rose is red, the leaf is green'.
WILL. A wench 'tis said Was found in your bed Beside the Queen.
QUEEN. God a mercy for that, Will, There's two angels for thee. I' faith, my lord I am glad I know it. . . .
EMPEROR. He's too hard for you, my lord, I'll try him. 'An Emperor is great, high is his seat, who is his foe?'
WILL. The worms that shall eat His carcase for meat Whether he will or no.
(*When you See Me You Know Me*, 1605) Sig. L.Iv.

There were simple jests with custard pies and pints of beer for gormandizing clowns. By the late 1590s, certain

sections of the audience were beginning to tire of this kind.
There is a passage in the Bad Quarto—the actors' version
—of *Hamlet*, that sounds like a warning. Hamlet is made
to say:

> You have some again that keeps one suit of jests, as a man is
> known by one suit of apparel, and Gentlemen quote his jests down
> in their tables before they come to the play, as thus: Cannot you
> stay till I eat my porridge? and You owe me a quarter's wages,
> and My coat wants a cullison and Your beer is sower, and blabbering
> with his lips and thus keeping in his sinkapace of jests when God
> knows the warm clown cannot make a jest except by chance as
> the blind man catches a hare.   (3.2.50ff.)

Compare Lavache's universal answer that fits all questions
in *All's Well* 2.2: 'Oh, Lord, spare not me' (which is
proved unserviceable by his mistress).

Tarlton, a robust and vigorous solo artist, improvisor
and swordsman, with a line in 'blue' jokes artfully pre-
tended to be much simpler than he was. After his death
in 1588, Will Kempe, a dancing and singing clown, had
taken the lead. He joined the Lord Chamberlain's Men,
and we know that he played Peter in *Romeo and Juliet* and
Dogberry in *Much Ado About Nothing*. But in 1599 he left
and it was then that Shakespeare met the congenial Robert
Armin, for whom he created Touchstone, Feste, the gravedigger in *Hamlet*, Lavache in *All's Well*, and the Fool in
King Lear.

The new feature about these parts is that they are
dramatically interwoven with the central characters and
the central feelings of the play; they demand an actor
ready to play many parts, not just his own brand of clowning. It is a mark of confidence that Hamlet can dismiss
the kind of clown who gags, and banish jigs and tales of
bawdry from the repertoire he wants; if the new clown
had liked such a style of acting, the lines would have
produced a backstage row.

Armin's style may be deduced from the rôles which
Shakespeare created for him; but there is other evidence,
for Armin was himself quite a prolific writer, though not
of any permanent significance. Nevertheless, it seems

curious that no one has looked at Armin's works, to try to
measure how closely Shakespeare was conforming to the
kind of humour that these shew to have been his speciality.
I am going to consider these works in some detail, because
I think they do throw light on Shakespeare's careful study
of his clown's particular style; but first, perhaps, a word
about Armin himself by way of introduction.

Robert Armin, son and brother of merchant tailors,
and grandson of a fletcher, was born at King's Lynn, four
years younger than Shakespeare; in 1581, at 13, he was
apprenticed for eleven years to a famous London goldsmith, Master of Works at the Royal Mint.[2] Socially the
Goldsmiths were a most exclusive craft; so Armin's
parents must have been fairly wealthy and he must have
been reasonably well educated. But next year his master
died.

There is a jest-book story that claims 'Tarlton made
Armin his adopted son to succeed him' because Armin,
sent by his master to collect a debt from a man named
Charles, who lodged with Tarlton, chalked up a verse on
the defaulter's wall.

> O world, why wilt thou lie?
> Is this Charles the Great! that I deny
> Indeed Charles the Great before,
> But now Charles the less, being poor.

Tarlton read the lines and added some of his own:

> A wag thou art, none can prevent thee;
> And thy desert shall content thee.
> Let me divine. As I am,
> So in time thou'lt be the same,
> My adopted son therefore be,
> To enjoy my clown's suit after me.

And see how it fell out. The boy, reading this, so loved
Tarlton after, that regarding him with more respect, he used to
his plays, and fell in a league with his humour; and private
practice brought him to present playing, and at this hour performs
the same, where at the Globe on the Bankside men may see him.
(*Tarlton's Jests*, 1611, ed. Halliwell Phillipps, 1844, p. 22)

Armin became a pamphleteer and player with Lord Chandois' troupe; he also seems to have given private performances. He probably joined the Lord Chamberlain's Men in the autumn of 1599. Next year there appeared his rhyming jest book, of which only one imperfect copy in the British Museum survives, under the pseudonym of 'Clunnico del Curtanio Snuffe'—Snuffe, the Clown of the Curtain Theatre—where, you will remember, the company had to retreat after the Theatre had been evacuated. (Later works appeared by 'Clunnico del Mondo Snuffe', the clown of the Globe.) The Italian style reminds us that Armin knew that language—he published some translations from it—and as for the name 'Snuffe' he signs the dedication to the reader 'Thine own Snuffe, that takes it in snuff, not to be well used'. This little work parodies academic disputations by the method of question and answer, the answer being itself deflated by a concluding 'quip'.[3]

The very form of the little book therefore puts Armin with learned fools in the great tradition descending from Thomas More, patron of players, and from Erasmus, rather than the boisterous clowns of the countryside and the playing place. He was a vivid, peppery, stimulating jester; yet also nervous if spirited, and rather waspish. If Erasmus' *Praise of Folly*[4] gave supreme wisdom to the Fool, we know that Armin saw the whole world as Folly's subjects: he opens his book with a return to the origins of man, his first question being 'Who first began to live i' the world?'

The full title of his little blackletter octavo is very revealing:

> Quips upon Questions; or a Clown's conceits on occasions offered, bewraying a moralised metamorphosis of changes upon interrogatories; shewing a little wit, with a great deal of will; or indeed, more desire to please in it than to profit by it. Clapt up by a clown of the town, in this late restraint, having little else to do, to make a little use of his fickle muse and careless of carping. By Clunnico del Curtanio Snuffe.

> Like as you list, read on and spare not,
> Clowns judge like clowns, therefore I care not.

or thus:

> Flout me, I'll flout thee, it is my profession
> To jest at a jester, in his transgression.

The mock dedication to 'His right worthy Sir Timothie Truncheon; Alias Bastinado, ever my part-taking friend' is an address to Harlequin's bat, and yet also a poignant reminder of the whippings and beatings that were the jester's lot both on stage and in great households. 'I salute thy Crab-tree countenance with a low congey being struck down by thy favour. Whereas I sometimes slept with you, in the fieldes, wanting a house o'er my head . . . guard me through the spittle fields I beseech you.' There follows an appeal to the Readers, ending with the famous 'Harlequin bow'—'Readers, revilers, or indeed what not, to you I appeal . . . and so a thousand times making leg, I go backwards till I am out of sight, hoping then to be out of mind'. But this does *not* end the very elaborate introduction; there is an old fashioned address of encouragement 'To the Book'.

There follow about forty questions, some ironic, some nonsensical, some sententious and some bawdy. This little catechism, with its mock academic form, shews how Armin enriched and changed the clowning tradition with rapid and nimble shifts of posture, acceptance of contradiction, flirts and fidgets of wit.

He had caught up, in his humble way, with the vogue of Paradoxes and Problems. The first question—'Who first began to live i' the world?' the answer being Adam, leads into a learned discussion of First and Last Men but ends with the 'quip':

> Thou art a fool. Why? for reasoning so.
> But *not* the first or last, by many mo.

Other questions include: Why barks that dog? who sleeps in the grass? who's dead? who's the fool now? what's near her? what's a clock? are you there with your bears? where's Tarlton? These presumably formed part of Armin's repertory in his one-man shews or after-pieces.

There are several anecdotes about the theatre. Some are about tumults and the robbing of simpletons, 'Where's Tarlton?' leads to the story of a simple Collier 'that knew not chalk from cheese' who, although he had heard Tarlton was dead, went to the play and demanded to see him.

> Within the play passed was his picture used,
> Which when the fellow saw, he laught aloud:
> A ha, quoth he, I knew we were abusde,
> That he was kept away from all this crowd.
> The simple man was quiet and departed,
> And having seen his picture, was glad-hearted.

This leads into a bitter little disquisition on fame, identity and survival: the play mentioned must be *Three Lords and Three Ladies of London*, in which the picture of Tarlton is used in a scene written to mourn his death.

A malicious jest 'Can that Boy read?' might have been directed on a member of the audience. The answer is 'Yes, he can read and write and cast accounts, and once his reading saved him from you-know-what'—a hanging. There must have been some moments when exchanges with the audience came near a David Frost show.

Armin himself was pathetically proud of his learning, and given to scraps of Latin. Shakespeare gives such a justifying tag to Feste: 'Cucullus non facit monochum, that's to say, I wear not motley in my brains'.

Erasmus quotes Cato about the wisdom of playing the fool in due season, and so does Armin. He ends his little catechism with an ample apology:

> Gentles, whose gentleness in censuring
> Is to take pleasure in your pitying:
> Craftsmen, whose craft in cleanly covering
> Is to be crafty in your kindest cunning,
> To you I appeal; to whom in my appealing,
> I crave forgiveness, giving this hard dealing.

Armin's first Question suggests not only Feste's song 'A great while since the world began', but the gravedigger's riddle about Adam in *Hamlet*. From the time that Armin joined the company Shakespeare very noticeably began to give his clowns the catechisms as a form of jesting. Touchstone questions Rosalind and Celia in this way, and proves the damnation of the country yokel by a catechism; Feste catechizes Olivia on why she grieves and proves her a fool for doing so; later, in the guise of the curate, he catechizes Malvolio. Lavache plays the same kind of game with

Robert Armin as Blue-Coat John, in his own play
Two Maids of Moreclacke

Helen and the Countess; the gravedigger uses it as his chief form of witticism. Lear's Fool uses riddles and questions to undermine or ridicule pretensions.

The very name of Touchstone is of course a reference to Armin's trade—the touchstone was the emblem of the goldsmiths, and the name is given to various characters who follow this trade, including the heavy father of *Eastward Ho!*

Armin took over Kempe's famous part of Dogberry, and was evidently proud to do so, for ten years later in a dedication he apologizes for 'the boldness of a beggar, who hath been writ down for an ass in his time, and pleads (under forma pauperis) in it still, notwithstanding his constableship and office'.

He was certainly not restricted to one line in clowning, for in his own play, *Two Maids of Moreclacke*, he doubled the parts of a clever servant Touch with that of a well known London character, Blue-coat John, a poor idiot who was kept at Christ's Hospital and became a kind of public plaything. There is one point in the play where Touch (played by Armin) has himself to disguise as Blue-coat John. As a dramatist, Armin must have caused some embarrassment to his new colleagues, for his play is one of the most confused, overcrowded farces of multiple disguise to survive from the Elizabethan stage. Two girls and their lovers outwit parental opposition with the help of Touch[5]: It is the playhouse equivalent of a curious knotted garden, a thick tapestry, or the intricate embroidery of a lady's state dress. That Shakespeare had read or seen this play is plain from the capital he makes out of one of its scenes. In Feste's opening scene in *Twelfth Night* he says

> I am resolved on two points.
> MARIA: That if one break, the other will hold; or if both break, your gaskins fall.

This quibble on the tagged points or laces of Elizabethan breeches would recall to the audience a scene where Armin as Blue-coat John had played counters with one of the blue-coat boys.

> JOHN. I ha' ne'er a counter.
> BOY. I'll give thee one for a point.
> JOHN. Do, and I'll play hose go down. (C.3.v.)

When John's nurse finds he had parted with the lace of his breeches she cries:

> I'll whip ye for it, take him up. Lose your point, lamb, fie! up with him, sirrah

and she slaps his bottom till he cries 'Good nurse, now, no more, truly, O, O.'

Nothing is more memorable than the clown getting a good thrashing, and this hilarious scene is what Shakespeare briefly recalls, to put the audience in the right frame of mind at the start.

Sir Topaz's talk about transmigration exploits another interest of Armin who, from Straparola's *Piacevoli Notti*, translated a fairy tale about shape-changers. Another little item from *Quips upon Questions* suggests why Sir Toby should go drinking in his boots—because either his shoes or his stockings are too disreputable to be seen.

There are several characteristics of the rôles of Armin which serve to distinguish him from the ordinary clown:

(1) He attends upon ladies, rather than on lords (Armin was devoted to Lady Mary Chandois and Lady Haddington). Touchstone, Feste, Lavache share this trait.

(2) He is often contrasted with a knave and he likes to prove that others are either fools, knaves or both, by means of catechism and other marks of the wise Fool.

(3) He underlines or calls attention to social gradations; although living outside the social order, he enforces it. (This is a characteristic of *Quips upon Questions*.)

(4) His wit is bitter and deflationary.

(5) He is given to music and song.

ii. Twelfth Night and the Reign of Fortune

But what Armin seems to have provoked in Shakespeare (and membership of the company in Armin) was the integrated comic vision of an Erasmus or a More of the world of fools; the idea of what Erasmus had first termed the 'foolosopher' (a word picked up by Armin). 'He uses folly as a stalking horse and under cover of that he shoots his wit' defines Touchstone, in words close to Armin's

SHAKESPEARE THE CRAFTSMAN

own definition: 'Fools natural, are prone to selfconceit/ Fools artificial with their wits lay wait.'

Feste is Malvolio's first and principal antagonist, parish clerk to Lady Folly.

He never uses such gross terms of familiarity as earlier clowns, but he can conjure money from old friends like the Duke or strangers like the twins; he invents wonderful mock authorities to edify Sir Andrew; he can parody the church service as readily as Erasmus himself.

Very early, he foresees the fate which overtakes Malvolio; 'God send you, Sir, a speedy infirmity for the better increasing of your folly' (1.5.172-3).

At the end Feste recognizes the rounded and absurd perfection of the comedy—'Thus the Whirligig of time bringeth in his revenges'. There was a feeling that the clown ought to be able to deal with anything—perhaps from his taking on all comers—and in *Quips upon Questions* a faintly discernible notion of some grand inclusive plan can be guessed by the opening question on Adam, and others on the state of the world. It is really a medley incorporating some traditional jests, including one of Tarlton's in answer to the question 'What's fit?'; some little tales; some pieties ('Where does the devil keep Christmas?') and some 'blue' jokes. The new kind of wit depended on being able to adjust to a varied audience, to play a multiplicity of rôles. The clown was losing his independence as an entertainer; he was no longer a challenger but a servant. As Viola recognizes, this asks sensitive responses to mood and company:

> This fellow's wise enough to play the fool;
> And to do that well craves a kind of wit:
> He must observe their mood on whom he jests,
> The qualities of persons and the times,
> And like the haggard check at every feather
> That comes before his eye.
> This is a practice
> As full of labour as a wise man's art.   (3.1.68-74)

No confident jig for such a character—he ends with a melancholy song. And in his next appearance a household

58

jester Yorick has long been dead, and Armin the clown is digging a grave. The association of the Fool and Death in the famous pictures of Hans Holbein had haunted Shakespeare's imagination since he wrote of the antic Death crouching within the hollow crown circling a king's brow (*Richard II*, 3.1.160-70).

Although his writings are broken and confused, and his history with the players too seems a broken and uncertain one, Armin's sympathetic *rapport* can be sensed in the full, gratified unity of conception that makes *As You Like It*, *Twelfth Night*, and *King Lear* each in so different a way macrocosmic, a complete world whose inhabitants live in a special glow, or light that suffuses them:

> Folly, sir, doth walk about the orb like the sun, it shines everywhere. (3.1.36-8)

Perhaps as he spoke, Feste glanced round the orbed seats of the Globe Theatre, with a bow that included the audience in this observation.

In *Twelfth Night* we are transported by way of an old English festivity (Twelfth Night was the occasion for masques, fantastic happenings, the last of the great Christmas feasts, followed by St Distaff's Day and Plough Monday) to a sunny Mediterranean land where it is always afternoon. Except for his versatile page, the Duke's household is shadowy but at the Countess Olivia's we see life below and above stairs. We seem to be in a city with an Elephant Inn, but Olivia's country-style living belongs outside the walls where Christmas was kept as Shakespeare knew it—by a big generous, noisy, rapacious court, with Christmas cheer for all comers. Summer and winter, city and country, an old world of revels and a new one of social distinctions are somehow all united—the only discord being in that ill-will which kills imagination.

To King Charles the play was known as *Malvolio*, and from an early admirer we learn that it was Malvolio the crowds went to see.[6] Van Doran says of Toby's attack on Malvolio, 'It is the old world resisting the new; it is the life of hiccups and melancholy, trying to ignore latter day puritanism and efficiency' and between his mood and the music of old manners it may be felt that Malvolio is 'dreadfully likely to prevail'. Certainly Olivia would not have this important and necessary officer miscarry for half of her dowry; but when he resents the quips of Feste, she diagnoses him acutely: 'O you are sick of Self-Love, Malvolio, and taste with a distempered appetite'.

Self-Love, as many authorities from Erasmus to Ben Jonson bear witness, is the chief attendant on Folly; and Folly, as again Erasmus and other authors had made clear, held her rule in the world of fools by delegation from Fortune, or Lady Luck. The unity of this play comes from the Rule of Fortune over the lives of Orsino, Olivia and the twins, and the Rule of Folly over life below stairs. As a victim of Self-Love, Malvolio tries to climb the wheel of Folly's Mistress, Fortune. 'All is Fortune' he remarks as he picks up the deceptive love letter from 'the fortunate-unhappy' (2.3.21). But it is Folly that guides him—the penalty of his aspiration to be Count Malvolio is to be taken for a madman; when all is revealed, Olivia tacitly withdraws her offer to let him judge his own case—'Alas, poor Fool, how have they baffled thee!' Malvolio's 'obedient hope' was not exactly madness—since the Countess does marry one whom she takes to be a serving man; moreover in real life, as perhaps some of the audience would remember, that formidable royalty, the widowed Duchess of Suffolk, had married her youthful Master of the Horse. Eworth painted the termagant beside the slight lad who is nervously fingering just such a jewel as Malvolio covets.

On the other hand the deception practised on Malvolio is certainly no more vindictive than the jokes courtiers played on each other (or on actors). Fools would treat rival fools with even greater violence—Armin describes one who half-killed and put out the eye of a rival.[7] The tricking of Malvolio was specially commended as a 'good practice' i.e. a clever deception by a young lawyer who saw the play given at Candlemas 1602 in the Middle Temple Hall. 'Flout me, I'll flout thee,' (remember), was one of Armin's mottoes.

The cross garters and yellow hose recommended to

Malvolio were those of the henpecked husband in a popular song. 'Malvolio's a Peg-a-Ramsey,' cries Sir Toby, and the chorus of this popular ditty was:

> Give me my yellow hose again,
> Give me my yellow hose,
> Forsooth my wife she follows me,
> See yonder where she goes.[8]

So Malvolio is drawn into the kingdom of folly. Ecclesiastes has said the number of fools is infinite, and the idea of a kingdom of fools was familiar in carnival and sottie. Malvolio in fact performs a kind of little play to his appreciative stage audience, and when he is bound in the dark room, Feste performs one of the regular clowning acts by holding a dialogue in which he sustains both parts, demanding that Malvolio subscribe to the heretical doctrine of transmigration[9] and in his own person challenging the devil, now inhabiting Malvolio, to combat.

Sir Toby, if he had been a different sort of person, would have been Olivia's natural guardian; old houses harbour such buffoons as proof of their own antiquity and dignity. 'Am I not consanguineous? am I not of her blood?' he protests: 'Tillyvally, lady.' He 'talks puffingly and explosively and is as full of wine as he is loud with song', but he belongs to a rough countrified society, and his place is below stairs with Fabian, who had got into trouble about a bear-baiting. Within the fantasy there is a very clear sense—an actor's sense, or a jester's—of precise social distinctions. The most poignant comes at the end of Feste's last song when he suddenly turns into Armin himself, as the wind and rain of January fall, the world returns to work again, ending foolish things and childish toys. For the Players' offerings, unlike those of the old households, *will* go on, as part of a workaday world.

> A great while since the world began
> With hey ho, the wind and the rain,
> But that's all one, our play is done,
> And we'll strive to please you *every day*.
>
> (5.1.417-20)

Here, the moment of comic truth is the moment when the old world of the revels turns into the new world of the theatre, and when the craft of the player is laid aside for a final bow as he turns to 'woo the twopenny room for a plaudite'. The new fool is a fool *deferring to an audience*.

The immediate effect of the play may have depended on Feste, but later King Charles was terming it 'Malvolio'. Such fools were out of fashion, and William Cartwright in 1647 dismisses them as part of Shakespeare's uneducated simplicity. 'Nature was all his art.'

> Shakespeare to thee [Fletcher] was dull, whose best jest lies
> In the ladies' questions and the fools' replies;
> Old-fashion'd wit which walk'd from town to town
> In turn'd hose, which our fathers called the Clown.
> (Verses prefixed to the Folio ed. of Fletcher, 1647)

For the fine social distinctions that are sustained by the world of love had been lost in the intervening years.

'Love and Fortune play in Comedies' had been an old adage of the stage,[10] and though the Lovers are partly in Folly's jurisdiction, they are ruled chiefly by her great Mistress, the Goddess Fortune.

In case it may be thought that such distinctions would not be immediately present to an ordinary attendance at the theatre, I should point out that there was quite a number of plays about fools in the years 1598-1604; that Armin's printer, William Ferbrand, brought out a number of books on fools, including one by Armin himself that categorized six different sorts of fool; and another that supplied fools culled from every county in England.[11] It would be possible to take *The Hospital of Incurable Fools* (1600) translated from the Italian of Tomaso Garzoni, and assign every one of the characters in *Twelfth Night* to one or other of the thirty different wards for different sorts of fool, each presided over by an appropriate God. Under the general patronage of Lady Fortune and presided over by Dame Folly, the Hospital would have accepted Malvolio among its 'malicious and despightful fools' who were placed for cure under the goddess Nemesis.

Some men there be that inwardly have inserted to them such
a spirit as if they happened at any time to be offended or injured
by any one, with a foolish wilfulness at one time they began to
contend with him. . . .
(The Thirteenth Discourse,
The Hospital of Incurable Fools, 1600, pp. 56-60)

Orsino and Olivia might be placed among the 'solitary
and melancholy fools', Toby as a 'drunken fool', Andrew
a 'dottrel and shallow-pated fool' or a 'carpet and amorous
fool' or perhaps even a 'gross and three-elbow'd fool'.
At all events he is more of a fool than anyone else.

Feste on the other hand would be placed among the
'parasitical and scoffing fools' of whom it is said that they
should not be enclosed in the hospital at all, but among
the wise and under the special protection of God Mercury.

In the dedication of this book, Cato and Erasmus are
joined as the upholders of wise fools.

The whole strength of Shakespeare's work lies in the
fact that it is not analytic but directly and fully dramatic
in its presentation. It does not carry even the amount of
argument and ceremony that belongs to his earlier plays
of the noble courtly life, still less such atrophied social
grading as Jonson's unsuccessful *Cynthia's Revels*.[12] But
on the other hand, the delicate relationships of Orsino,
Olivia and Viola will reward the closest inspection; they
are fully personal while fully dramatic. The Duke opens
the play

> If music be the food of love, play on:
> Give me excess of it, that surfeiting
> The appetite may sicken and so die.
> That strain again! it had a dying fall.
> Oh, it came o'er my ear like the sweet south
> That breathes upon a bank of violets,
> Stealing and giving odours. Enough! no more,
> 'Tis not so sweet now as it was before.   (I.I.I-8)

In eight masterly lines, you have the tragi-comic Duke;
absorbed in the sensation of love, he yet wants to be rid of
it. The lines are so beautiful that one overlooks the suppressed violence that would kill by satiety. A susceptible

young Italian who hardly wishes to know the beauty whose image drives him from one 'shape' of fancy to the next, he is exquisitely sensitive to the perfume and suppliance of a minute and to the fine variations of his own

Fortune favouring an ape

mood ('O spirit of love, how quick and fresh art thou!'), only to feel an immediate recoil. 'Now the tailor make thy doublet of changeable taffeta,' says Feste, 'for thy mind is a very opal.' This was a recognized state of lovesickness;

the duke is meant to be a little mad—agreeably so, but perceptibly off-balance. Yet his servants tell us he is not inconstant in his personal favour to them. And with Cesario he becomes frank, sceptical, mocking, for of course, quite unaware of what is happening, he is falling in love more reasonably and on the way to a cure.

Viola is changeable as the Duke is, but changeable because she is so ready to adjust to Fortune's whims; it is these, not Folly, that toss her about. She remains charmingly prepared to laugh at her own predicaments, plays at being Sebastian, in fantasy restoring the brother she had lost by taking his shape. He was seen binding himself to a mast as their ship went down—'courage and hope both teaching him the practice'; Viola too, with courage, hopefulness and a readiness to improvise, accepts her unwelcome mission, while perfectly clear about her own wants.

> Who e'er I woo, myself would be his wife.   (1.4.42)

She puts on an inflated style like a bad player

> Most radiant, exquisite and unmatcheable beauty—I pray you, tell me if this be the lady of the house, for I never saw her, I would be loath to cast away my speech, for besides it is excellently well penned, I have taken great pains to con it. (1.5.160ff.)

Olivia gives the expected cue for such a 'happening'; 'Whence came you, sir?' and Viola breaks decorum again; 'I can say little more than I have studied and that question's out of my part'. 'Are you a comedian?' asks Olivia with a touch of scorn, and Viola disclaims the professional rôle, which nevertheless colours all the scene. After Olivia has unveiled the face which is Orsino's 'Heaven on earth', complacently asking 'Is't well?' the whole thing is deflated by the cool 'Excellently well, if God did all!'

Then when the young messenger strikes the true note, as she remembers what it is to feel the soul by love drawn out into another's being, she moves out of her jesting, living her part so effectually that Olivia is carried away too, suddenly overwhelmed by a part of herself she does not know. 'I do I know not what' she says, 'Our selves we do not owe', and from mourning, she is plunged head over heels in love with mockery and courage.

The whole situation being resolved by the appearance of the twin, the play ends like a square-dance. The miracle of the twins (it is described theologically)[13] dissolves that unreal inner world, where the Duke had lived tormented by fancy and Olivia by her own loneliness. Faced with a snub in public, the Duke grows maddened by the 'ingrate' rejection of his 'devotion'. He knows he must kill somebody and knows he loves both Cesario and Olivia.

> I'll sacrifice the lamb that I do love
> To spite a raven's heart within a dove.
>
> (5.1.134-5)

The formal Petrarchan images make it quite unreal, but Viola hears him say he loves her, and she cries at once:

> And I most jocund, apt and willingly
> To do you ease, a thousand deaths would die.
>
> (5.1.136-7)

At the end of comedies it was usual for a heroine to be exposed to an alarming risk; in one of Peele's plays, she is threatened with being sawn in half. Here we have all the conventions—'A duke there is, and the scene is Italy as those things lightly we never miss'—but now, when Orsino learns the very worst treachery, he is suddenly jolted into sanity. There is no more talk of killing when he thinks Olivia and Cesario married; take her, he says, but don't let us meet again.

And finally he is left with laughing, stumbling efforts to disentangle the boy Cesario from a new image that is beginning to form—his 'fancy's Queen'.

All the elements of control in the story—the suffusive power of Fortune and Folly, the 'Italianate' compliments and the device of the twins—do not distract attention from the natural aspects of festivity and character as they evolve here.

'What's to come is still unsure.'

The comic vision was more elusive than the tragic, but

in *Twelfth Night*, it is fully embodied. To attribute this to the presence of a gifted clown rather than the presence of an Italian Duke (as Leslie Hotson would have it in *The First Night of Twelfth Night*) implies that Shakespeare had left behind that ceremonious kind of drama which he perfected in *A Midsummer Night's Dream*, and that he was as deeply influenced by his fellow-actor as by his audience. A momentary compliment, a skilful improvisation might be part of the play; but the play itself had become a craft mystery.

Twelfth Night, because it was made for one company at one time by a master of craft carries the self-adjustive elasticity of all great drama; being so complete and beautifully balanced in itself between the world of revels and the January cold, it absorbs the imbalance of those who would present or accept it.

That the solution to a dramatist's problem, which had been puzzling the stage since Sidney had complained of Clowns, should be a practical matter—a matter of temperaments and of occasion—is what might be expected of this social art. Even as the play succeeded in London, at Cambridge students were still shewing a clown drawn in on the end of a rope and told to extemporize:

> Clowns have been thrust into plays by head and shoulders ever since Kempe could make a scurvy face . . . if thou canst but draw thy mouth awry, lay thy leg over thy staff, saw a piece of cheese asunder with thy dagger, lap up drink on the earth I'll warrent thee they'll laugh mightily. . . .

The difference between this and the kind of inconsequence that Feste may shew in a begging plea to the Duke ('the bells of St Bene't may put you in mind sir, one, two, three') is the difference between Nature and Art; but, 'the Art itself is Nature'.

iii. Armin's Later Career

Shakespeare gave to Armin the form which Armin was not capable of giving himself; what can be seen in his

SHAKESPEARE THE CRAFTSMAN

works is the shadow of it. There was some fragile timidity, or some deep-seated melancholy in Armin which meant that he could not sustain his own writing or his acting for long. In *Quips upon Questions* he speaks of wandering about and sleeping in the fields, and the work breaks off:

> Ere the middle came, weariness took him,
> So that his Muse, offended, quite forsook him . . .
> Weakness of wit was cause he did so bad,
> Not love of heart, for that was always had.

Sometimes he 'sleeps in the grass' on the way to his Lord's house at Hackney; in time of plague, such things may happen. But Armin may really have had some impulse to wander and to shift his way of life. The very different lengths of the parts assigned to him in Shakespeare's plays and the irregularity of them suggest that he was the temperamental kind of actor that every company likes to have but finds it hard to hold down. The gravedigger scene is important for the whole conception of *Hamlet*, and in exchanges between Burbage and Armin over the skull of the dead jester (and both would have known Tarlton) the tragedian may have learnt a new dimension for tragic musings. The Porter in *Macbeth*, the Old Man in *Antony and Cleopatra* are almost as brief parts as the Fools in *Othello* and *Timon*—where a momentary sinister appearance strikes a discordant note to happy fortunes. Armin was included in James's Letter Patent of 1603 which constituted the King's Men, but he was not a shareholder in the Globe or the Blackfriars; the actor Phillipps who died in 1605 left him only a small remembrance, and in his own will, Armin termed himself a goldsmith and did not leave any remembrances to the players at all.

Was he still working as a goldsmith for part of the time, or living with a patron? He was not poor; his brother was a merchant tailor of the city. But Feste and the Fool in *King Lear* combine with what we know of Armin's own life to suggest a touching and rather frightening picture.

68

Though like Will Summers, King Henry's fool, Lear's fool sleeps among the dogs, and knows the habits of Lady the Brach, he contradicts in his behaviour the shrewd and bitter wisdom of his 'foolosophy',

> I will tarry; the fool will stay,
> And let the wiseman fly:
> The knave turns fool that runs away,
> The fool no knave, perdy.   (2.4.83-6)

While Lear remains in contact with the world of society, the fool clings to him, but in the regions of the wolf and the owl, he is replaced by Tom-a-Bedlam, Edgar in his antic disposition; so he forms a minor assistant in the trial scene and departs with the mysterious paradox 'I'll go to bed at noon'.

A shrewd ironic professional, but also a little cracked, the fool bears an instinctive knowledge of Lear's misery and remorse, but though his emotional connexions are always right, his intellectual connexions are often wrong —hence his mistimed jeers at Goneril. Mentally unstable persons can often achieve great emotional intuition, but being terrifyingly imperceptive of their audience, their comments, like those of children, may be intolerably apt and completely misplaced. The fool, Lear's pet creature and almost a part of himself, shares none of Feste's power to observe on whom he jests; his magic wisdom belongs with the upside-down world of the storm.[14]

As early fools are shewn devoted to the good things of life, especially food and drink (many of Armin's stories are about the fool's tricks to gain quince pies or cream) so the practical, beggar's cunning of Lear's fool makes his fidelity more heroic. As he stands locked outside the castle gate he achieves what Erasmus had regarded as the singular blessedness of fools, a kind of contentment, in his piteous echo of Feste's song:

> He that has and a little tiny wit
> With a heigh ho, the wind and the rain,
> Must make content with his fortunes fit,
> Though the rain it raineth every day.   (3.2.74-7)

Though we do not see the fool with Cordelia we know of his devotion to her; it may not be irrelevant to recall that in a dedication to Lady Mary Chandois, Armin says

> Your good honour knows Pink's poor heart, who in all my services to your deceas'd kind lord, never savour'd of flattery or fiction.

In Armin's own play, Touch is turned out of service for fidelity to his young mistress and is threatened with hanging as well as whipping:

> Gang is the word and hang is the worst, we are even, I owe you no service and you owe me no wages, short tale to make, the summer's day is long and winter nights be short, and brickill beds does hide our heads as spitall fields report. (D.I.v)

Feste recalls that 'he that is well hanged need fear no colours,' 'and for turning away, let summer bear it out' (1.5.5-6, 19-20).

Armin published more on Fools as his parts grew. His *Fool upon Fool* (by Clunnico del Mondo Snuffe) describes six famous fools. Leonard the lean fool is a horrible creature 'the base son of Envy' some of whose tricks are extremely malignant; but Jack Miller 'the clean fool' is an endearing character who wept when he was praised and laughed when he was beaten. Jack Miller loved the players.

> Lord Chandois' players came to towne and used their pastime there, which Jack not a little loved, especially the clown, whom he would embrace with a joyful spirit and call him Grumball, for so he called himself in Gentlemen's houses, where he would imitate plays, doing all himself, king, clown, gentleman and all; having spoke for one, he would suddenly go in and again return for the other, and stammering so beastly, as he did, made mighty mirth. (*Works*, ed. Grosart, p. 28)

His master shut Miller up in a locked room so that he should not stray after the players, but he climbed out and crossed a frozen river on the ice to reach them. As a punishment for this dangerous escapade his friends the players decided to beat him; he asked only that he should be beaten by his special friend Grumball the clown and took his beating with laughter.

With sudden presumption, however, Armin decided to turn philosopher and he reissued this collection of stories at this time with an Erasmian dialogue between the World and the Fool. To cure the World's sickness the Fool moralizes upon all and sundry; the critic and the world finally have a quarrel. This work Armin addressed to the gentlemen of the Inns of Court and Universities, but evidently they did not take it all kindly. His dedication asked that they would 'beautify our GLOBE in every line' so perhaps he meant to recite some of this dialogue. Poor Snuffe, taking it in snuff to be mocked, dedicated his next work, to Lord and Lady Haddington, with a great deal of hoity-toity grandeur and some Latin flourishes. It is a fairy tale about rival magicians, in which the apprentice sorcerer, after turning himself into a horse, a fish, a ruby ring—in which form he wins the love of a Princess—persuades his irate master to become a cock, then turns into a fox and gobbles him up. Ballad stuff? not at all, protests the author.

> Cameleon-like, thy mind misgives
> All colours like thine own . . .
> Conclude in charity, thou fool
> That thinks thyself most wise,
> Thy wit's not worthy any school,
> 'Tis salt and too precise.

In 1615 there appeared an anonymous play, *The Valiant Welshman*, which is sometimes attributed to Armin; it reads as if composed by a drunkard who had been learning Armin's parts. There are confused recollections of Gloucester, Cornwall and the Bastard from *King Lear*, a close parody of the gravediggers' scene, there is a Roman ravisher who steals into the bedroom of a sleeping British Princess. The hero, presented as one of the Worthies, rescues the king in the disguise of a poor soldier, vanquishes whole armies; a witch and her son, inhabitants of a cave, are paired with a magician who can go invisible.

The only one of Jonson's plays in which Armin's name appears in actor-lists is *The Alchemist*, and in *The Valiant Welshman* there is a scene where a poor fool is cheated of all his clothes by being told the fairy queen is in love with him —an exact imitation of Dapper's scene.

Given all this, and the fact that author says at the end he had to stop because he didn't know how to finish but if anyone wants some more he will go on, I would think that Armin might well have been responsible for this appalling piece of gibberish. If so, it would certainly not have endeared him to the King's Men. The play has an Induction from Fortune, who raises up from an ancient tomb a Bard, the purported author of the play; this retains all the old craft spectacle with all the old craft confusions. This most old-fashioned kind of chronicle, signed only R. A., was the property of Alleyn's company, coming in print in 1615.

Armin had made his will in December 1614, and it was proved in November 1615. He described himself as Citizen and Goldsmith of London; he left his goods to his wife Alice, with remembrances to his nephew, brother and sister; omission of his fellow actors seems significant. The will was drawn in the hall of Mr Armin's house, and the inventory of his goods fixed at £160; he was buried in St Botolph's, Aldgate as 'goldsmith and player'.

Armin is probably the first actor whose career indicates the advantages and disadvantages of a temperament; the contrast between the ephemeral quality of his own literary remains and what he inspired in Shakespeare cannot disguise the likeness between the man behind the one and the other.

If Burbage made possible the circumstances in which Shakespeare developed his dramatic range, Armin may claim a humbler but still a memorable place amongst those whose talents furnished something towards Shakespeare's use.

Many nostalgic tales had grown up round the royal jesters of earlier days, and the alleged power that they exerted at court. Skelton, supposedly a jester to Edward IV,

Scogan to Henry VII and Will Summers, court jester of
Henry VIII, represented the wishful power of the plain
man at court, nearest of all to the king. In all early plays the
King and the Fool were seen in close relation to each other;
both were magic figures, carrying suggestions of larger
powers. When the Oxford students put on their merriment
A Christmas Prince, in the same year as *King Lear*, they
made Stultus the last and most faithful of the deposed
Prince's followers.

John Davies of Hereford, in his *Scourge of Folly* begins
his collection of worthies with King James and ends it with
a wise fool—Robert Armin. He may be the last of the
series—and this in itself links him with the first—he may
be compared with a skipping flea, 'that tickles the spleen
like a harmless vermin', yet he is distinguished from lesser
men of the same sort.

> And so much more our love should thee embrace,
> Sith still thou livest with some that die to Grace,
> And yet art honest in despite of lets,
> Which earns more praises than forced goodness gets.

The conclusion carries an unexpected link with the opening:

> So thou, in short, the happiest men doth school,
> To doe as thou doest, wisely play the fool.

The people's nickname for King James was 'the wisest fool
in Christendom'. He kept at his court his Scots jester
Archy Armstrong, and Middleton, late in his reign, could
write:

> There's nothing in a play to a clown, if he
> Have the grace to hit in't; that's the thing indeed;
> The King shews well but he sets off the King.
> *(Hengist King of Kent*, 1618, 5.1)

But with the disappearance of Armin from the stage, the
line of great stage fools and jesters also ended. Like his
grandfather, the fletcher, he belonged to a dying craft. He
profoundly modified what he had inherited but he could

73

not transmit his ways to the next generation. 'Like the bells of St Bene't's one, two, three' the three great artists Tarlton, Kempe and Armin succeed each other.

Next, we turn to a new kind of comedy, *The Merry Wives*.

CHAPTER V

ROYAL COMMAND:
THE MERRY WIVES OF WINDSOR

TO look at a beautiful old piece of craftsmanship you need to know just for what sort of people it was designed, and how they were to use it. The message will be there, in the curve of a wooden handle on a short sickle; the worn and moulded shape of an old leather jackboot tells of limbs long under the earth. How a glove is frayed—how the legs of a joint stool are worn—how the pages of the orchard scene from *Romeo and Juliet* were thumbed over by the first generation of Oxford scholars who read it—this is evidence, but it may need careful interpretation.

The craftsman's 'form' is learnt in the process of making, by innumerable examples, not by recipe and precept. He works like a good cook. 'Take of fennel and cast in enough' say those maddening cookery books of Shakespeare's time. Familiarity and habituation; the long maturing of a seven years' apprenticeship made a craftsman.

The craft of making poetry and of making plays had long been familiar to Englishmen. It was a 'gentle' craft—like woodcraft or working fine metals. It was not difficult to see how the various kinds of play or game fitted snugly into the spring time or harvest festivals; how the actual feel of the summer day or the winter firelight had gone into the work and made it fitted for that occasion and that only.

In conversation recently (I hope he will not mind my repeating it) W. H. Auden roundly asserted that *The Merry Wives* was Shakespeare's worst play. Perhaps this is understandable from a lyric poet—for this is the most prosaic drama Shakespeare wrote, rising only to very pedestrian verse. Its virtues are craft virtues.

An experienced man of the theatre, John Dryden, on two separate occasions singled it out for praise as the first regular play in English;[1] by this he meant of course that it observed the 'mechanic beauties' or craftsman's rules of his theatre—the three unities of time, place and action. And William Oxberry in 1820, writing as actor and artist said, 'this delightful comedy is perfect, if the term perfection can be applied to any creation of human genius'.[2]

Without attempting immediately to reconcile the contradictions, I shall consider *The Merry Wives* as an example of craftsman's theatre—a special order carried out superbly with all the resources of a great playwright and a great company. The very early tradition that it was written in a fortnight at the command of Queen Elizabeth, who wished to see Falstaff in love, explains both the strength and the limitations of what is one of the most thoroughly professional jobs in the English theatre.

Such a request would be most exceptional. There is no evidence that plays were ever specially commissioned for court; the players brought along their repertory. A gorgeous masque or shew might be put on by a nobleman or the gentleman of the inns; but mounting a play was a very expensive business, and by the turn of the century players would not be prepared to do this for the kind of honorary reward that they got from the Court—the chief reward being of course prestige and advertisement. It is said that Queen Mary never paid more than £5 for one of her celebrated toques, because she considered the value of her custom made this reasonable; Queen Elizabeth I upheld the same principle.

Public performances brought in the money, but the players justified them as rehearsal 'to do her Majesty service'. A royal command would have represented a flattering attention; no greater compliment could have been paid by the Queen than personally to give a theme. Perhaps from Shakespeare's view an impossible theme; Falstaff in love! But what—faced with the order—did he do? We might ask, as of any other piece of craftsmanship, what is it made of, how was it put together, what is it used for?

In this play, it may be hazarded, we see what Shakespeare did when pushed hard. He turned out, most supremely competently, a planned, tidy, lively serviceable play which enjoyed professional esteem throughout the seventeenth century, and which has held the stage continuously both in England and elsewhere. It is translatable, and so has also enjoyed a special vogue in Eastern Europe; Verdi made it into a great opera. Simply to be as sure of what you were doing as that in 1600 was a most remarkable accomplishment.

(This date I would maintain in spite of Leslie Hotson on account of the relation with *Henry V*, which can scarcely be earlier than 1599; and also because of the vogue of city plays which followed in the early years of the seventeenth century.)

In my second chapter, on Shakespeare's company of players, I suggested that during the plague of 1592-4 Shakespeare may have taken refuge in a country house, as other playwrights did, and have written *some* plays specially for performance in such surroundings. *Love's Labour's Lost* and *Midsummer Night's Dream* require more boy actors than a public company had—and must therefore have relied on choristers or schoolboys to fill out the cast. The whole atmosphere and address of the plays relates to a small group of privileged spectators, and both, by the interpolated shews, mock the art of playing.

The Merry Wives of Windsor represents quite a different approach to a special audience—the compliment to the Queen is inserted almost by way of epilogue in the final masque, and for the rest the play is a confident offering from a world *outside* the court, a world that is almost precisely that of the little country town where Shakespeare had centred his claims to gentry and good standing and where he was already by 1600 well established as a leading citizen.

On the other hand as a piece of craftsmanship it is the product of a successfully established theatre, and one that was increasingly independent of court favour, surviving on the demand of the common citizens for this form of entertainment. It was no longer necessary to hold the mirror up to courtly life; we have moved from the world of Castiglione and Sidney into the new century.

But the old mock-battle between actor and audience underlies the treatment of Falstaff; there is a kind of covert hostility that culminates in the folk-game which is also a court masque, the hunting of the 'male deer' at Herne the Hunter's oak.

The play opens with a walk-on of figures some of whom do not appear again, for Act I is a shew parade of rôles from the company's recent comic successes—Falstaff and his followers. The last act offers a kind of masque, employing a large number of child actors. These were presumably little choristers from the Royal service, available on this special occasion. Perhaps it was their very success in this shew that prompted the children's master to try them out on the London stage again. Between the actors' parade and the choristers' masque lie three acts of farce where Falstaff romps with the Merry Wives.

In the parade come Shallow and his Wise Cousin, a new figure modelled on Andrew Aguecheek, Pistol, Bardolph and Falstaff's Boy; Corporal Nym comes from *Henry V*; the company's Welshman had a part. What action there is in Act I concerns three men wooing a maid (there is a jig called *The Wooing of Nan*) and an absurd duel, both of which could be in the mind of the author from *Twelfth Night*.

At the beginning of Act II, the play suddenly bursts into life, as the confident and resourceful wives encounter each other with identical love letters. No woman can fail to feel flattered by a love letter and Mrs Page is at first amused—'What, have I 'scaped love letters in the holiday time of my beauty and am I now a subject for them? let me see' (2.1.1-3); but her indignation is roused by the attempt to carry her by storm and her dignity reasserts itself. Mistress Ford recognizes the social condescension implied and achieves an epigram; 'If I would but go to hell for an eternal moment or so, I might be knighted'. This hinted at the darkness of the act, and perhaps there is a naughty pun in *hell*[3] for the wives are free-spoken. 'These knights will hack' (stab, or ride any horse to hand), replies Mrs Page, to which her neighbour retorts with a proverb 'We burn daylight; there, read, perceive how I might be knighted'.

Rejecting the courtly code of secrecy in favour of bourgeois solidarity, the two women jump to the unromantic truth when they compare the duplicate letters with those duplicate dedications with blank spaces for names, which needy authors hawked about among subscribers. Falstaff would put us two in the press, says Mistress Page, but 'I had as lief be a giantess and lie under Mount Pelion' (2.1.81-2). Other brisk and familiar comparisons confirm the spirit of the formidable pair, and establish them as successors to a long line of tradesmen's wives, going back through Lydgate's Christmas mumming of henpecked husbands to Mrs Noah.

'Why, I'll exhibit a bill in the Parliament for the putting down of men', cries Mrs Page in the first flush of her wrath: 'what an unweighed behaviour hath this Flemish drunkard picked, with the devil's name, out of my conversation, that he dares in this manner assay me? Why, he hath not been thrice in my company!' (2.1.20-32).

Fortified equally by their wealth and their piety, the wives enlist Mrs Quickly as their courier. She, it appears, has never met Falstaff before; indeed she is much more like Juliet's nurse. Against this triple league, the wit of Falstaff has no chance. Though that thorough feminist Margaret Duchess of Newcastle applauded the whole plot as original, it is completely traditional in idea:

> One would think he [Shakespeare] had been metamorphosed from a man to a woman for who could describe Cleopatra better than he hath done, and many other females of his own creation as Nan Page, Mrs Ford, Mrs Page, the doctor's nurse, Mrs Quickly, Doll Tearsheet and others too many to relate.[4]

Once the main action of man wooing two women is set going, Falstaff's retinue disappears, Justice Shallow dwindles, peaks, and pines in the wings, the three men wooing Nan Page patter on in minor scenes as an underplot. Anne, we are told, 'speaks small like a woman' but the

Wives, especially Mrs Page, the more forcible of the two, speak very roundly. 'I cannot tell what the dickens his name is'—'Hang the trifle, take the honour', 'You do yourself mighty wrong, Master Ford'—these are not parts for boys. On the Elizabethan stage older women were played by men, and these are the star parts of the play, designed for leading actors. Here are the three first panto-mime dames, as it were; if they were not used to trans-vestite parts, it would have been all the more of a romp. The fun can be much more robustly enforced if these are men dressed up—a triumvirate set upon poor old Jack is a strong working majority. The scenes would carry the spirit of a jig, providing both a challenge and a jollification for the leading actors of the Lord Chamberlain's Men.

Finally of course Falstaff becomes a transvestite himself when he escapes from Ford's house (but not his cudgel) in the guise of the old fat woman of Brainford.

It would be nice if the Old Vic followed its all-male *As You Like It* with an all-male performance of *The Merry Wives*.

In the Bad Quarto, an actors' version of the play, even the masque is made farcical, because there were not enough boys to play it; the part of the Fairy Queen is given to Mistress Quickly, and Sir Hugh appears as Puck; he gives satiric charges to Bean and Bead, to deal with the City police.

> Go lay the Proctors in the Street,
> And Pinch the lowsy Sergeant's face
>
> (Q.1., 5.5.55-6)

The terrified modesty of Master Slender, which forbids him even to accept Anne's politely urged summons to come in to dinner, contrasts with the blitzkrieg of Falstaff; as his letter moves from a polite 'you' to a familiar 'thou', his arm can be felt sliding round the ample waist.

> Ask me no reason why I love you. . . . Let it suffice thee, Mistress Page, at least if the love of a soldier can suffice; that I love thee. I will not say, pity me, 'tis not a soldier-like phrase; but I say, love me. (2.1.4-14)

'What a Herod of Jewry is this,' cries Mrs Page, amused but not impressed. She recognizes the bad, out-of-date play-acting, as well as the stupendous wickedness of such an assault upon her by no means infantile innocence; and at once begins the counteraction.

The women's league in one form or another is an ancient source of comic dread. 'If your husbands were dead, I think you two would marry,' says Ford to Mrs Page; the reply is at her tongue's end 'Yes—to two other husbands'. There are two hunting games afoot in the play; the women's league are hunting ... Falstaff, while he and Master Ford, mutually deluded, are in their different trails hunting Ford's wife. 'If I cry out thus upon no trail, never trust me when I open again' (4.2.212) exclaims the leader of the men's pack who comes to turn his own house upside down. The peppery and oath-besprinkled speech of Dr Caius, the mercurial variety of Parson Evans, and the super-confident bellow of Mine Host are designed for a full range of vocal effects by a practised team, with the shrill piping of Silence and Shallow for the tenor.

Hunting, coursing, birding are the chief occupations of the play—we never learn the trades of Ford or Page; indeed they seem more likely to be merchants and bankers, as it is their gold that attracts Falstaff. In the Bad Quarto, even Dr Caius inadvertently talks about his 'counting house' instead of his 'study'. Incidentally, the most likely way for Shakespeare to have heard stories about the celebrated Caius was from a young Cambridge graduate who, after studying medicine elsewhere, had just come to take up residence at Stratford. Shakespeare's future son-in-law, John Hall, may have known that the third founder of Caius College had such an antipathy to Welshmen that he forbade their admission to his foundation—but the idea of making Caius into a Frenchman could have come from John Hall's mixed reminiscences, and Shakespeare's own matchmaking efforts with his Huguenot landlord in London.

Although Shakespeare may not (as yet) have been concerned about his own daughter's marriage, yet in 1600 she would have been seventeen—just about the age of sweet Anne Page; and she was Shakespeare's heiress. If Shakespeare wanted to found a family, the identity of Susannah's husband was of critical importance. In this play, the anxious parents are defeated, and Falstaff has the satisfaction of feeling that his downfall has contributed to theirs:

> I am glad, though you have taken a special stand to strike at me, that your arrow hath glanced.   (5.5.259-61)

Master Fenton, the companion of the mad-cap Prince of Wales, comes to Falstaff's rescue—Fenton with the gay bachelor's buttons (or buttercups) sprinkled like a May Lord's fancies on his courtly finery:

> Embrouded was he, as it were a meede,
> Al ful of fresshe floures, whyte and reed.
> Syngyinge he was, or floytynge al the day;
> He was as fressh as is the month of May
> (Chaucer, *Prologue*, 89-92)

Such a young man is born to success, as the Host proclaims (and there is more than a touch of Chaucer's Harry Baily about the Host).

> He capers, he dances, he has eyes of youth, he writes verses, he speaks holiday, he smells all April and May; he will carry't, he will carry't, 'tis in his buttons; he will carry't. (3.2.71-4)

The wooing of Nan follows a traditional theme for citizen comedy. Shakespeare's old rival Greene had shewn an earl wooing the keeper's daughter at Fressingfield, with the Prince of Wales as rival (*Friar Bacon and Friar Bungay*). Shallow's opening complaint: 'Knight, you have beaten my men, killed my deer and broken open my lodge' is countered by Falstaff's cool taunt 'But not kissed your keeper's daughter? . . . I have done all this' (1.1.115-20). The zest of the hunt, the fast instinctive move of hounds on the scent, drives the play forward, though it is a human hunt up to the last scene where Falstaff impersonates the ghostly Hunter; then, he who boasted to give the horns becomes the hunted prey. Dragging a chain like a lugged bear he goes 'like Actaeon, he, with Ringwood at his heels', not only the ghost of the old hunter but the ghost of himself.

Wooing games and roving in the woods, the mad mistakes of a night, were a popular and traditional subject for many plays, and here again the actors had as it were a craft model upon which basis they and their dramatist could work.[5]

The humours of the wooers and the mad mistakings which surround Mistress Anne leave her cool and always ready to 'be herself' on her own terms. When Fenton admits that her father thinks his interest is mercenary and he loves her 'but as a property', Anne observes with penetrating candour 'Maybe he tells you true' (3.4.11). She remains outside the women's league (or should it be called the Women's Institute?) 'Never a woman in Windsor knows more of Anne's mind than I do,' boasts Mrs Quickly —and that is precisely nothing. Anne has appealed in vain to her mother against being married to Caius, under the sexually vivid image of feeling herself a mere property, a target for country sportsmen to aim at:

> Alas, I had rather be set quick i' the earth,
> And bowl'd to death with turnips. (3.5.90-1)

Youth and age are in contest from the beginning and youth wins. The old man turned young by love is mocked; 'Youth in a basket!' snarls the furious Ford, thinking he has found his victim, and at the end Falstaff is mocked as 'metamorphosed youth'. He in turn feels himself a cockshy, beringed by little William and his shrill-voiced mates:

> See now how Wit may be made a Jack-a-Lent when 'tis upon ill employment! (5.5.137-8)

The Jack-a-Lent or popinjay was a ragged figure used as a target; Falstaff's diminutive page, Robin, suggests the image to Mistress Page, as she takes him away firmly from what would have undoubtedly developed into a career of juvenile delinquency and promises the 'little Jack-a-Lent' a new doublet and hose (3.3.27-8).

For Robin, like Falstaff, has strayed into another world than the one he was born to. Falstaff in love! an invitation to ridicule which effectually dictated the level on which the Queen wished to be entertained. She did not ask for fine sentiments. But Falstaff, as theatrical creation, had proved such a success that all London was inventing new scenes for him. Lady Southampton wrote to the Earl:

> All the news I can send you that I think will make you merry is that I read in a letter from London that Sir John Falstaff is by his mistress Dame Pintpot made father of a goodly miller's thumb, a boy that's all head and very little body. But this is a secret. (*Shakespeare Allusion Book*, vol. I, 88)

and Sir Charles Percy down in Gloucestershire played the part of Justice Shallow.[6]

The original Falstaff of course could not be revived. He had developed, perhaps without conscious planning; his heart had been 'fracted and corroborate' by Hal's denial of him. However in the world of the theatre, no death is final; the impossible but intensely flattering order was manfully obeyed. The players met their day, and fulfilled their service and humble duty. Falstaff was brought out of the wardrobe—tatters, padding and all—only to be dumped back into the property basket. For that most serviceable object at last came into its own—what is the buckbasket but the property basket with the contents of the players' wardrobe? Other players have found other uses for it—Dame Sybil Thorndyke, in World War I, is said to have brought her babies to the theatre in case of air-raid warning and to have popped them in the property basket when she went on stage.

The relish with which Falstaff recounts his adventure among the laundry is the relish of his creator at seeing the old rags come to life. Told first to Bardolph, then to the deluded husband, the narrative rings with the built-in irony of the Gadshill story. To Falstaff, however, it is by now all as good as a play, though broken off when 'we had embraced, kissed and as it were, spoken but the prologue of our comedy'.

I suffered the pangs of three several deaths; first an intolerable
fright, to be detected with a jealous rotten bell wether; next,
to be encompassed, like a good bilbo, in the circumference of a
peck, hilt to point, head to heel; then to be stopped in, like a
strong distillation, with stinking clothes that fretted in their own
grease; think of that, a man of my kidney, think of that, that
am as subject to heat as butter; a man of continual dissolution
and thaw; it was a miracle to scape suffocation. And in the height
of this bath, when I was more than half stewed in grease, like
a Dutch dish, to be thrown into the Thames, and cooled, glowing
hot, in that surge, like a horse shoe; think of that, Master Brook.

(3.5.101-117)

The suppressed response of the listener to this makes a
silent dialogue, as Ford learns how he has been cheated, and
yet also how he has been avenged. And another chance
comes to Ford: 'he cannot creep into a half penny purse nor
into a pepper box'. The wives in their imagination enact
the scene to themselves:

What a taking was he in when your husband asked who was in
the basket! I am half afraid he will have need of washing.

(3.3.190-3)

In his transvestite rôle as Old Mother Prat, Falstaff gets
the sort of beating that Evans was always promising un-
willing scholars, but afterwards he boasts to the Host that
an old woman 'hath taught me more wit than ever I learnt
before in my life, and I paid nothing for it neither but was
paid for my learning'; and to Ford, more openly, of his
own histrionic skill 'my admirable dexterity of wit, my
counterfeiting the action of an old woman', which delivered
him from the cudgel and the stocks (4.5.122-6). The
vivacity and creative zest of his tormentors has been stimu-
lated also; they set on again. 'Come,' cries Mrs Page, 'to
the forge with it then; shape it; I would not have things
cool!' (4.2.242-4).

These jests are the familiar stuff of classical comedy of
Figaro and Goldoni's innkeeper. The story indeed has a
long ancestry, mainly in Italian plays; Boccaccio, Ser
Giovanni Fiorentino (whom Shakespeare had used before),
Straparola's *Piacevoli Notti* (which Armin was to translate)

and a collection of jests that were put out under the name of Tarlton the Clown.[7]

The Italian works, and many of the English comedies derived from them with likenesses to Shakespeare shew one startling difference—

All are tales of *youthful* and *successful* adultery. None has more than one heroine; the cornuto may be an ancient professor, and the successful intruder one of his own undergraduates. This is the sort of comedy Falstaff imagines himself to be part of, with his scornful description of 'the peaking cornuto, her husband', and his own assumption of youthful energy. It is astringent; indeed, Machiavelli's *Mandragora* is a play of this kind.

Images of monsters haunt Ford—he invites the company home to dinner with the promise that 'I will shew you a monster' (3.2.85) and one does not know if it is Iago's 'beast with two backs', or himself as cornuto that he thinks of.

'Gentleman, I have dreamed tonight, I'll tell you my dream' (3.3.169-70) plays with the idea of a play, but when Falstaff reasures him 'Master Brooke, you shall cuckold Ford,' he cries to himself: 'Ha, is this a vision? is this a dream? do I sleep! Master Ford awake! awake, Master Ford! there's a hole made in your best coat, Master Ford!' (3.5.228-31; 4.2.131-5).

He feels himself the ragged object of public derision, while his friends interpret his 'imaginings' as madness. In Italian stories, the cornuto is sometimes actually confined as a madman by his malicious wife.

Mistress Page thinks Falstaff and lovemaking go together as well as the Hundredth Psalm to the tune of Greensleeves, but in the new and moral interpretation of a bawdy tale, *she* provides something much more like Greensleeves to the tune of the Old Hundredth.[8]

In the forest scene it is, of course, Falstaff who is admitted to the order of Cornuto, by incorporation as it were. Draped in his leg chains, he also provides a kind of parody of the Garter ceremony.

The village mumming of the Hunting of the Wild Man,

the old German folk-play, may lie at the back of the legend of Herne the Hunter; there is a cruel folk ritual here where the wild man is lured to death by a woman (a part played by another man in disguise).[9] But at Windsor too there would be a theme of the transformation of Actaeon in the presence of Diana (Ovid was in Shakespeare's mind, as one or two phrases betray). Diana duly received her praise in the final masque: at one point Falstaff seems to dissolve the play world and speak directly to the original audience— the court, who are always just off-stage in the play, but who were actually in their seats in the auditorium:

> If it should come to the ears of the court how I have been transformed and how my transformation hath been washed and cudgelled, how they would melt me out of my fat drop by drop and liquor fisherman's boots with me; I warrent they would whip me with their fine wits till I were as crestfallen as a dried pear.
>
> (4.5.97-103)

So, in the final scene, imagination in chains stands under the pelting invective of shrewd counting-house and pulpit in Puritan alliance:

> MRS PAGE. Why, Sir John, do you think . . . that the devil could ever have made you our delight?
> FORD. One that is as slanderous as Satan?
> PAGE. And as poor as Job?
> FORD. And as wicked as his wife?
> EVANS. And given to fornications and to taverns and sack and wine and metheglins? (5.5.158-171)

The ingredients of the play so far have turned out to be the old traditional triumph of the women's league (the Hock Tuesday play), the pastoral wooing of courtier and country beauty, the merry mistakings of Love in a Wood, and jealous Italian comedy, revised to a moral English theme. There remains what might be called the social comedy or comical history and here again Shakespeare has used and transformed an old stage convention.

In comical histories, the King always appears in festive association with his subjects, and often in disguise. The prototype is the meeting of Richard Coeur de Lion and Robin Hood, with their mock fight. Edwards or Henrys are received by the keeper of Fressingfield, by George-a-Greene at Wakefield, by Hob the Tanner of Tamworth, by the mad Lord Mayor Simon Eyre in London.[10] No monarch appears or is even mentioned in this play about Windsor town—for the Queen had commanded it and was present at its first performance.

'It was not for me to bandy compliments with my sovereign,' said Dr Johnson on a like occasion; the great honour made any intervention of royalty in the play unnecessary—except the 'reflector' rôle of the Fairy Queen in the mask. The most graceful thing was for the players to keep within their own sphere, and this was what happened. Indeed, it can happen today. When Her Majesty gave a party at Buckingham Palace for Shakespeare's fourth centenary, the very famous actors and actresses who attended dressed with extreme restraint, respectability, almost dowdiness. Glamorous ladies of the footlights appeared like members of the Mothers' Union—which they probably are. Glamour was provided by the setting, the Guards, the Band, and the hostess. The actors were not competing.

In this play, and in this play alone, we meet Shakespeare at home. The occasion, the compliment, called out a modest civic pride. Bernard Shaw was probably right, when he wrote *The Dark Lady of the Sonnets*, in suggesting that William Shakespeare was rather proud of being the son of the High Bailiff of Stratford.

We meet the whole of a small town society here; it is not just sketched in by one or two figures, but presents the crowded vivacity of a Breughel painting, with many little sideshows. Of course this is a holiday society. Even little William is given a holiday from school, the burghers spend their time in sports; there are bears in the town.

Relations however are realistic, not idyllic. The play is solidly and comfortably bourgeois; it belongs to the new society of late Elizabethan times. Mistress Ford, when the court was at Windsor, had been the subject of attention from 'Earls, nay which is more, pensioners' but she scorned them all. Mistress Page leads a better life than any in Windsor: 'Do what she will, say what she will, take all, pay all, go to bed when she list, all is as she list' (2.2.223-4), according to Mistress Quickly, who adds that she never misses morning and evening prayer. (Traditionally, of course, this was a way of making assignations; but that comfortably-placed grass widow Mistress Anne Shakespeare would have enjoyed freedom even from the need for this subterfuge.)

This is a pious community, and Ford repents in the language of religion—for which he is rebuked by the solider Page.

> Now doth thine honour stand,
> In him that was of late an heretic,
> As firm as faith.   (4.4.8-10)

Mistress Page not only appropriates Falstaff's last remaining servant, but is inclined to bully the schoolmaster (under the formula, well known to all instructors of youth, 'My husband says . . .'). She does most of the planning for the Falstaff campaign, enlists Quickly, arranges times and seasons; but Mistress Ford commands a deadly coolness of retort, appropriate to one who had domestic difficulties, that is just as serviceable as Mrs Page's more authoritative dominance.

> 'Three or four families in a country village is the very thing to work on.'[11]

as a later comic artist counselled; the scene at Windsor is very close to the scene at Stratford. It has already been suggested that the arrival of an eligible young physician may have reminded Susannah Shakespeare's parents of the problems that they would expect to meet in the next few years.[12] Here is Stratford on Avon's open hospitality; the hard shrewd look cast at a stranger; the small boy being led to school; the Welsh schoolmaster (Shakespeare's master had been Thomas Jenkins); the distant sound of barking dogs as the bearward leads in his blind shackled charge. Ben Jonson knew the streets of London in this way; what Shakespeare knew best of all was 'English verdure, English culture, English comfort, under a sun bright, without being oppressive'. There are no beggars, no handicraftsmen, no Wart nor Bullcalf; only the upper crust of small-town society, with its personal servants.

Shakespeare had bought the largest house in the town, acquired a coat of arms, and seems to have acted a sort of banker and general agent for his Stratford friends when he was in London. In Stratford he would seem a gentleman of leisure, and his London connexions would be a source of pride and not of mixed pride and scorn.

The Merry Wives of Windsor gives, as no other citizen's comedy does, the feel of provincial society at a particular time; there is an exact awareness of the attitudes and prejudices of a prosperous, Protestant, moralizing citizenry that is almost Jonsonian. For instance, Master Page rejecting the courtly suitor of his well-endowed girl:

> Not by my consent, I promise you. The gentleman is of no having . . . No, he shall not knit a knot in his fortunes with the finger of my substance. If he take her, let him take her simply; the wealth I have waits on my consent and my consent goes not that way. (3.2.75-82)

When a man is hard pushed, he will employ what is nearest to hand and uppermost in his mind. The solid prosperous citizen and the man who wrote the 90th Sonnet:

> Then hate me when thou wilt; if ever, now;
> Now while the world is bent my deeds to cross,

were one and the same because this Protean author lived in divided and different worlds, and had, perhaps at very great cost, learnt to do so.

Here, he gives the detail of life in a country town, presented of course in a rosy light. For that reason, I cannot but think that the vast volume of commentary upon the social background of this play is almost completely mistaken.

The two favourite topics for those who try to interpret this play—and some have shewn very great learning—is whether in the opening lines of the play, the remarks about

Justice Shallow's coat of arms—'the dozen white louses is an old coat'—refer to some personal enemy of Shakespeare; and whether in a very obscure jest about some German horse thieves he were mocking the Duke of Württemberg K.G., a rather eccentric nobleman who, after many petitions, was given the Order of the Garter in 1597.

It used to be thought that the dozen white louses referred to Sir Thomas Lucy of Charlecote, who according to earlier legends had tried Shakespeare for deer stealing, and whose coat of arms included three luces—or pike.

This legend probably grew out of the play itself, for there was no deer park at Charlecote till Jacobean times. Then Professor Hotson identified the coat as that of Mr Justice Gardiner[13]—who quartered the Lucy arms—an unpopular character with whom Shakespeare appears to have had some differences, for Gardiner and his nephew swore the peace against Shakespeare in November 1596.

This joke about the 'dozen white louses' as a coat of arms comes in the very opening lines of the play, before the audience has really got settled down at all. It seems that only an ignorance of social occasion quite unthinkable in the Lord Chamberlain's Men would lead them to begin a play at court with private jests against characters who were certainly not in the court orbit. Those who imagine Queen Elizabeth or the Lord Chamberlain would enjoy jokes against a Surrey justice or a Warwickshire knight, or who think that Shakespeare would have given enemies this kind of publicity cannot have paused to reflect on the social structure of Elizabethan England.

There is one piece of coat armour in the play that everyone would wait to see. That had better be a comic one. The coat armour of Falstaff—ragged and preposterous—would appear on his surcoat. His followers likewise, until they were discarded, would wear badges of some kind, although they were clearly 'leaders of thousands'. I think this jest is a preparation for the entry a few lines later of the lousy coats of Falstaff and his men, probably with some absurd badge. Mock-heraldry was an old and long standing joke of the players.

Now the relevance to the 'Jack-a-Lent' appears, and Ford's cry 'There's a hole in *your* best coat, Master Ford' may be taken to reflect directly upon the apparel of his rival.

Elsewhere, on the Bankside, a jest against the unpopular Justice Gardiner might have had some point; and in opposing Gardiner it appears that Shakespeare had the support not only of the owner of the Swan Theatre, a solid citizen, but two stout-hearted dames of the neighbourhood.

An Offering at Court would naturally culminate in a compliment to the Chief Spectator. This form Shakespeare had practised in *A Midsummer Night's Dream*, which leads up to the blessing of the house and the bridals. Here the masque in Windsor Forest leads up to a reference to the great Windsor ceremonies of the Garter Knights. The Fairy Queen commands the elves to bless Windsor Castle.

> Strew good luck, ouphs, on every sacred room,
> That it may stand till the perpetual doom,
> In state as wholesome as in state 'tis fit,
> Worthy the owner and the owner it.
> The several Chairs of Order look you scour,
> With juice of balm and every precious flower,
> Each fair instalment, coat and several crest
> With loyal blazon evermore be blest!
> And nightly, meadow fairies, look you sing
> Like to the Garter's compass, in a ring;
> The expressure that it bears, green let it be.
> More fertile fresh than all the field to see;
> And *Honi soi qui mal y pense* write
> In emerald tufts, flowers purple, blue and white;
> Like sapphire, pearl and rich embroidery,
> Buckled below fair knighthood's bending knee;
> Fairies use flowers for their charactery.   5.5.63-82

This speech is perfectly in keeping with such passages as the epilogues at court, written by Jonson for *Every Man out of his Humour* or Dekker for *Old Fortunatus*; it is omitted in the popular abbreviated version which came out illegally in 1602, when the part of the Fairy Queen is satire and is given to Mistress Quickly.

But in a play which contained this kind of compliment, it would not be tactful for the players to mock anyone on whom Elizabeth had just bestowed great honour, however ridiculous he may have been, nor to insinuate jests about Germans who indulged in horse stealing.

There *is* a little joke about German horse stealing in the course of the play—one of those little sideshews that it was customary to provide, like side-dishes at a great feast, an obscure detail in a great Breughel panorama.

By misleading Anne's suitors about the rendez-vous for their duel, Mine Host of the Garter incurs the wrath of both Caius and Evans (who is forwarding the cause of Master Slender). Later we hear that three Germans have put up at his inn; they ride off to court to meet a German duke without paying, and are seen no more. The news is brought simultaneously to the Host by Evans and Caius that there are cozeners abroad and that in fact no German duke is expected at the court. Each adds 'I tell you for goodwill'—and vanishes forthwith.

Now this trick of bringing bad news to an enemy and adding 'I tell you for goodwill' is a stock stage trick, which can be found elsewhere.[14] For an actor the brief effect of two former enemies popping their heads round the door simultaneously, delivering their news and vanishing is quite enough after we have heard them plan a joint revenge on the Host:

> I desire you that we may be friends and let us knog our prains together to be revenge on this same scall, scurvy, cogging companion, the host of the Garter. (3.1.120-24)

Caius replies 'By gar, vit all my heart'. As to the jest itself, there is one, that would serve, in *The Merry Jests of George Peele*; horse-stealing is the common theme of the jest books, and even Master Slender could have provided an instance out of the *Hundred Merry Tales*. Horse-stealing leads up to the far more important wife-stealing, in which, once again Caius and Master Evans's protegé are cozened by the Host and Master Fenton.

93

In the satiric version of the play, meant for the general public, the Doctor says

> Dear be a Garmaine Duke come to de Court
> Has cozened all de host of Brainford
> And Reading, I tell you for good will,
> Ha, ha, mine Host, am I even met you? (4.5.88-91)

to be followed by Evans:

> There is three sorts of cozen garmombles
> Is cozen all the Host of Maidenhead and Readings
> Now you, are an honest man and a scurvy beggarly lowsy
>   knave besides:
> And can point wrong places,
> I tell you for good will, grate why my Host. (4.5.79-83)

There *may* be a reference here to Count Mömpelgart, later Duke of Württemburg, but this is simply the sort of thing that clowns put in when they speak more than is set down for them. The incidental 'glance' or 'hit' of this kind is essentially a popular one, and last summer at Stratford, Ontario, I heard such a gag—the most successful gag I have ever heard in Shakespeare. Jean Gascon, the present Director and a French Canadian, was playing Dr Caius. At the end of the last scene when he finds that instead of Anne Page he has married 'un garçon' Caius made a splendid storming exit—'By gar, I raise all Vindsor!' but on the exit he turned, and in the very voice of the President of the French Republic whose recent visit and pronouncements had caused such a political storm, he added—'And zat is an insult to La France!'

The applause was tumultuous.

The Quarto version is altogether a good deal more malicious. Mistress Ford rather pertly twits Mistress Page, Falstaff is not let off the twenty pounds he owes Ford. This version is generally supposed to have been supplied to the printer by the actor who played the host. (Anyone who reported his own line after the taunting of Evans and Caius —'Hue and cry, Bardolph!' as 'Hugh, and coy Bardolph' must have had his tongue loosed by drink.) The real attraction was not the wooing of Nan, as the title page makes plain.

> A most pleasant and excellent conceited comedie of Syr John Falstaff, and the Merrie Wives of Windsor. Entermixed with sundry variable and pleasing humours of Syr Hugh the Welsh Knight, Justice Shallow and his wise Cousin Master Slender. With the swaggering vein of Ancient Pystoll and Corporall Nym. By William Shakespeare. As it hath been acted by the right honourable my Lord Chamberlains servants. Both before her Majestie, and else where.

Of course it was acted elsewhere. Another play on Falstaff, and one which had been given by royal command would be a perfect goldmine for the company.

The structure certainly shews some marks of haste, in the early parade of the safe Shakespearean humours of Falstaff and his rout. At the beginning it may be meant for a comedy of masters and servants. Simple and Jack Rugby, the servants of Anne's two foolish suitors, might have turned into Tranio or Dromio. Simple is hidden in a closet by Mrs Quickly; his cozening by Falstaff's men is another little side-shew that is never fully worked out, but it is recalled when Simple turns up in Falstaff's lodging to consult the Wise Woman of Brainford.

I would think that in this play, working at speed, Shakespeare made use of a 'Factotum'—a roughly familiar shape, which represented a speedy adaptation from stock. But I do not think that he took an old play, whether the lost 'Jealous Comedy' or the much more unlikely *Two Merry Women of Abingdon* and rewrote it. The last thing actors would want would be to relearn lines they already knew with slight modifications. The process I envisage is something like that Mrs Page suggests behind Falstaff's love letter:

> I warrent he hath a thousand of these letters, written with blank spaces for different names, and these are of the second edition. (2.1.75-6)

Once however, the play developed, with the transvestite farce of the Wives, other false starts were simply left un-eliminated. The play was designed to give a chance to all the company; everyone had a good fat part. This constituted its great charm for the comedian Oxberry, whose praises have been already mentioned:

> The play is to be tried as a whole, not by the value of a single character. . . . It is a composition of the highest order, in which light and shade are blended with matchless skill. Each character is admirably calculated for the display of those around it, and the various persons act on each other with the reciprocity of the various parts in a landscape.

In such generous and careful provision for all the company, this is no less a social play than in the modest realism which takes us outside the gate of the royal park, away from the courtly fantasies of *Love's Labour's Lost* to the society of Jacquenetta, Costard and Dull.

'Our fellow Shakespeare' provided the script; Burbage stepped down from his Falstaffian eminence to be cozened by two others; what came out was a synthesis of many theatrical genres which we do not recognize because they no longer separately exist.

Perhaps for once Shakespeare also took a quick look at the work of Ben Jonson. If the play was celebrated throughout the seventeenth century as being Shakespeare's only regular comedy, the only one to fulfil the classical unities, it is perhaps an ironic touch that in such circumstances he found they had their uses. All this adds up to the very best second-best Shakespeare—the side of him that was sometimes defeated by his imagination. *The Merry Wives* has the deceptive simplicity of the completely professional accomplishment.

CHAPTER VI

THE LIVES OF THE NOBLE ROMANS: JULIUS CAESAR AND OTHER ROMAN HISTORIES

THE view from the South Bank, where the Globe lay, is not at all the same as the view from the original Theatre; in a grand panorama the City lies spread out to view on the curve of the Thames. Such perspective and inclusiveness as that of the great engravings is found in *The Tragedy of Julius Caesar*, which Thomas Platter, a Swiss visitor, saw at the new theatre in 1599 as he records in his diary:

> After lunch on Sept 21st, at about two o'clock, I and my party crossed the river, where in the house with the thatched roof we saw an excellent performance of the tragedy of the first Emperor Julius Caesar, with about fifteen characters; after the play, according to their custom, they did a most elegant and curious dance, two dressed in men's clothes and two in women's.[1]

Without a jig, even the dignity and splendour of 'fifteen characters' would not please the groundlings; yet with a new kind of perspective *Julius Caesar* achieved a new freedom and liberation from the assumptions that had governed Shakespeare's art.

The play was, and has ever since remained, a great theatrical success. It is drama for the boards. In the nature of the subject, the handling of the speech and action, boldness and confidence in discarding the expected forms reveals itself, not by *statements*, but by the craftsmanship with which complex group relations are worked out in the first modern political drama of the English stage.

To change from English to Roman history, was to turn from a society threaded with deep emotional implications, combining religious symbolism and personal allegiances, to a City power-structure of patricians and plebs, governors and governed, whose impact from their own relation with the City of London could have seemed familiar to the players.[2] In his earlier writing on Rome, *Titus Andronicus* and the *Rape of Lucrece*, Shakespeare had used the Roman Kings and Emperors at their most tyrannical for stories of atrocity and extreme violence—a perspective by which he could contemplate the utter destruction of innocence, the white hind in the tiger's claws. Both works are highly formal; the violence is contained within a rigid frame. In his English histories, with growing complexity of 'mutual relations within society', conflicts of hierarchy and community are shewn in scenes that are sometimes historically distanced and at other times—in Shallow's orchard, for instance—purely Elizabethan. There are two time clocks (at least) in *Henry IV*. Although it is Shakespeare's particular glory to refrain from theorizing, to give problems embodied in behaviour, in *Julius Caesar* he is enabled to reflect looming dangers for which as yet there were no conceptual terms, for which even Machiavelli and Bodin did not provide the necessary tools. The political conflicts of the seventeenth century in England resembled more closely the struggle within a *polis* than the dynastic conflicts of the Wars of the Roses, and the first indications of these strains might have been felt—though they could not be defined—by the sensitive before the end of Elizabeth's reign. The citizen was less of a subject, the community less of a hierarchy. In moving away from legends centred on the court to something more like struggles within the City Council, the struggle of lesser crafts against the greater, Shakespeare brought in such mundane questions as legacies and payments, concentrated wealth, hard bargaining, yet without reproducing the life of everyday. On the contrary, anything which was given a Roman setting was thereby augmented, made grander, more didactic and intellectual, more heroic and dignified. To counterpoint the 'Black' City Comedy of crime, in *Julius Caesar*, *Coriolanus* and *Timon of Athens* Shakespeare provided a City Tragedy—which sometimes comes close to 'Black' Comedy, especially in the last two plays.

In my first two chapters I tried to give an impression of the long development that culminated in the Elizabethan theatre, and in Shakespeare's English Histories; the development of the company that he helped to establish as the central factor in the Reformation of the English stage. In the next two, the growing flexibility and strength of his own dramatic tradition in the period when the Globe was founded. In the last two chapters, keeping to this same narrow range of time, 1599-1601, I shall try to shew the great creative leap represented by his development in tragedy, with some sense of the future consequences, the perspective of Jacobean Shakespeare.

The emblematic value of the stage structure as visible Icon itself may have remained physically the same at the Globe as at the Theatre, but it was no longer *used* in the same way. It is said that supernatural beings cannot cross running water. When the players came to the Globe they effectually left behind certain qualities of the old playing place with its associations—those so eloquently described by Kernodle:

> For centuries, Kings had been presented to the public whether real kings in public ceremonies, or actor-kings in plays and pageants, in a throne backed by a symbol of the realm. That symbol combined elements from the city gates, from triumphal arches, from the choir screens of churches. The throne was framed by columns supporting a canopy or 'heavens'—exactly the same kind of pavilion canopy was used to frame an altar or a tomb. Heavenly singers proclaimed the praises of the heavenly kings and often a figure of God sat on a heavenly throne to endorse the earthly king below. The Elizabethan stage had absorbed all these medieval symbols. Its background structure resembled a castle a throne, a city gate, a tomb or an altar; it was a symbol of social order and of divine order—of the realities between man and king, between heaven and earth.
>
> (G. R. Kernodle, *Shakespeare Survey* 12, 1959; 'Open stage; Elizabethan or Existentialist?')

The murder of Julius Caesar eliminated this ancient Icon, as far as Shakespeare was concerned. (A beautiful example may still be seen by anyone who will look at the Gate of Honour at Caius, the perfect model of a traditional

SHAKESPEARE THE CRAFTSMAN

triumphant setting.) The chief occasion when it was again used by Shakespeare was in the bitter mockery of Macbeth's coronation banquet.

In these later plays, too, we meet a new conception of the gild—the faint suggestion, in the banding of the 'occupations' of the City, that the minor craftsmen retained their old unity but that the lords and merchants formed another political group. T. F. Reddaway has described the delicate relation between the City and the gilds in London at the close of Elizabeth's reign:

> In the governaunce of their craft, the (gilds) were supreme . . . in matters of law and order of defence, of supplies of food and water, of public health—of all that lies within the term of local government as we understand it today . . . the City ordered and the companies complied.[3]
>
> (T. F. Reddaway, 'The Livery Companies of Tudor London', *History*, vol. 61, 1966, pp. 287-99)

For example, it was the City which ordered the gilds to buy corn against dearth, and store it, an incident Shakespeare uses in *Coriolanus*.

The shift from craft to mercantile ventures meant that while the outward splendour and ceremony of the ancient gilds remained, the enormous population explosion in London, the growth of the suburbs, and new power-centres like the Royal Exchange indicated a transfer of authority, not yet institutionalized, but perceptible none the less. With a corresponding increase in violence and crime: London was the only English city with an underworld.

Those who have watched our local shift of power from colleges towards the university and the central planners will not want an analogue.

Shakespeare made a heroic attempt to compass a general statement in *Troilus and Cressida* which deals with the highest symbol of secular disaster, the Fall of Troy, archetypal City. Great political debates shew a mind wrestling with thoughts that 'dodge conception'. The debates of the Greeks on the nature of government and the Trojans on the springs of political action are contradicted by the events that occur; there is the same dislocation between creed and conduct, the same brilliant and blinding juxtaposition of their incompatibility in the story of the siege as in the story of Troilus's love.

Here Shakespeare also shews within the microcosm, the little world of man, ironic distortion and defacement of a great poetic ideal. He went to the greatest poem on human relationships that had yet been written in English—Chaucer's *Troilus and Criseyde*—and following it closely, deflated the tender and heroic story. What Shakespeare did to *Troilus and Criseyde* I have discussed elsewhere[4]; the poet's personal version of social confusion is mirrored in this most searching tragic drama, possibly not written for the public stages.

By contrast, *Julius Caesar* handles what was long considered the greatest crime of the Roman world, in a play of overt challenge and debate linked to clear action, whose dilemmas are set out with Roman clarity, Roman simplicity. It is a masculine play, not only because it treats of *respublica* but because it is written in a thoroughly masculine style. It commands great theatrical assurance, although its theme is betrayal. Its style is the nearest Shakespeare ever came to writing like Bernard Shaw.

Consistency within the variety of its rhetorical style evidences the craftsmanship of this play. It suggests the effect of a learned tongue—not the Ciceronian rotundities once so admired, which were now going out of fashion, but the 'brief compendious style' for which Plutarch praised Brutus, together with a more emotional rhetoric, Antony's 'Asiatic style'. In spite of his small Latin and less Greek, Shakespeare knew the feel of a classical language and could use in poetry such condensed pithy phrasing as Bacon had employed in the *Essays*, which stands in the very sharpest contrast to the florid doublings and the encrusted imagery of *Troilus*; witness two scenes of mental conflict.

> Things small as nothing, for request's sake only,
> He makes important; possess'd is he with greatness,

And speaks not to himself but with a pride
That quarrels at self-breath; imagin'd worth
Hold in his blood such swollen and hot discourse
That 'twixt his mental and his active parts
Kingdom'd Achilles in commotion rages,
And batters down himself.

(*Troilus and Cressida*, 2.3.181-7)

Between the acting of a dreadful thing,
And the first motion, all the interim is
Like a phantasma or a hideous dream;
The genius and the mortal instruments
Are then in council; and the state of man,
Like to a little kingdom, suffers then
The nature of an insurrection.

(*Julius Caesar*, 2.1.63-9)

Or these two moments of farewell:

Injurious Time, now with a robber's haste,
Crams his rich thievery up, he knows not how:
As many farewells as be stars in heaven,
With distinct breath and consign'd kisses to them,
He fumbles up into a loose adieu,
And scants us with a single famish'd kiss,
Distasted with the salt of broken tears.

(*Troilus and Cressida*, 4.4.42-8)

BRUTUS. Whether we shall meet again, I know not.
Therefore our everlasting farewell take!
For ever and for ever, farewell, Cassius!
If we do meet again, why we shall smile:
If not, why then this parting was well made.
CASSIUS. For ever and for ever, farewell Brutus.
If we do meet again, we'll smile indeed.
If not, 'tis true this parting was well made.

(*Julius Caesar*, 5.1.115-221)

Suspense is one of the predominant emotions in *Julius Caesar*; for the raising of suspense an exact control of language is needed. Shakespeare had used this before—in *Richard III*, where the conflict is given through sharpened use of dialogue; in *Richard II* where beautiful and extended images recreate that older sacramental world of kingship which is to be shattered like a mirror.

The whole of *Julius Caesar* is enclosed in a skin of rhetorical address, supple and elastic. In the forum scene, the process is boldly revealed to the audience as they follow the effect of Brutus and Antony on the crowd; it is an example of what I. A. Richards termed *Intention*, felt pressure of directing purpose moulding the speech. But everywhere in this play, the style is the man; Caesar always speaks as if he were addressing a public meeting; Cassius is hot and choleric, Brutus cool and insufferably in the right on all occasions; Casca affects bluntness. All exemplify the art of shewing in evolution thought and feelings 'as they rise in the mind'—this in itself belongs rather to the new century, as that great student of style F. P. Wilson observed:

> What distinguishes the Jacobean age from the Elizabethan is its more exact, more searching, more detailed enquiry into moral and political questions, and its interest in the analysis of the mysteries and perturbations of the human mind.
>
> (*Elizabethan and Jacobean*, 1945, p. 20)

Mobility of thought, feeling and response is reflected by the contrast with Latin brevity, and finality. Many writers have noticed that the whole action of the play begins to reverse itself immediately after the murder of Caesar with the entry of a servant—the messenger from Octavius who comes to Antony. With the entry of this man, his sudden sight of the murdered body, and his single exclamation—

O Caesar!

Antony is moved to weep but also to set in motion his plan, to 'try' how the people will react to the sight of Caesar's corpse. So throughout the play the arrival of a messenger, the sleepiness of a child servant, or the sudden irruption of a crazy rhymer acts as a catalyst for feelings that are being held back in suspense. And this build-up is masterly, in the deepest sense it is classical.

Although Ben Jonson, naturally felt it his duty to criticize Shakespeare, he was obviously impressed, for the great senate scene in *Sejanus* depends on exploiting just these qualities of style.

Plutarch's *Lives of the Noble Greeks and Romans* not only provided Shakespeare with new themes but with social

Fortune at her Wheel

conflicts of the kind which a dramatist must have found irresistible. History is seen in terms of great men, but their lives are artfully contrasted to bring out the underlying principles, a method naturally dramatic. For this particular play, the Lives of Caesar, Brutus and Antony, which were all relevant, gave slightly different perspective to the great events. The tense moments on the morning of the assassination and the scene of assassination itself are presented with chilling simplicity and Shakespeare adds only an extra stroke or two to deepen and clarify the effect; for example when Artemidorus presents Caesar on the very steps of the Capitol with the scroll revealing the names of the conspirators, it is Shakespeare who makes him put it by with the royal if presumptuous gesture: 'What touches us ourself shall be last served'.

Now this little incident had been stressed in that early Elizabethan model of political orthodoxy, *The Mirror for Magistrates*; a work which is a summary of late medieval tradition about the Fall of Princes.[5] But in *Julius Caesar*, Shakespeare makes a decisive break with medieval tradition, in a direction highly significant for all his subsequent

Many-handed Fortune

work, and a break with the underlying tragic concepts that informed all stories about the Fall of Princes, Fortune's Wheel, and Instability of Worldly Favour. It is very difficult to suggest the immense significance of this change without launching into empty generalities; so, returning to the early stage, and its concrete presentations as a means of radical simplification, I shall term it, The Canonization of the First Deadly Sin and the Displacement of a Goddess.

The Canonization of the First Deadly Sin, which is Pride, was achieved by the Roman doctrine of stoic autarky, the culmination of which was the justification of suicide: to a Christian, suicide was forbidden.

The goddess is the Roman Fortune, favourite of medieval tragedians, who by Christian stoicism had been converted into the Mover of the Wheel, ruler of sublunary events. She presides over Chaucer's great love tragedy, and also over much early Elizabethan Tragedy, which derived from The Fall of Princes or The Mirror for Magistrates. Shakespeare transforms her to her favourite aspect of Opportunity; no longer a tyrannical or hostile power, she is the embodiment of what the world can offer to man under the fleeting aspects of Time. Mutability is no longer

Occasion — 'there is a tide in the affairs of men'

necessarily evil. In that instant, his foot on the steps of the Capitol, Caesar, balancing the scroll, holds the future of himself and the conspiracy in his hands. The conspirators crowd round with their rival petitions, the moment is lost. Later, Brutus was to give full formulation to this existentialist choice, in metaphor that depends on time and bold venturing, even at the moment when, like Caesar, he dooms himself by his free election to take the field.

> There is a tide in the affairs of men,
> Which taken at the flood, leads on to Fortune;
> Omitted, all the voyage of their life
> Is bound in shallows and in miseries.
> On such a full sea are we now afloat,
> And we must take the current when it serves,
> Or lose our ventures.   (4.3.217-23)

106

Implicit in such a passage is the denial of perhaps a thousand years of determinism, in which man saw himself as helplessly bound to the wheel of Fortune, the great wheel of the universe, on which every human creature may rise only to fall again. This image of Fortune had been derived from Boethius; it had sustained Chaucer.

Fortune and her Wheel featured in many medieval pageants and games[6]; in George Gascoyne's play of *Supposes* (1566) the last dumb shew presents Fortune riding in a chariot drawn by four noble persons. On her right walk two kings, on her left two slaves; she stays the chariot, crowning the slaves and putting the slaves' rags upon the Kings.

When Marlowe's Tamburlaine boasts that he holds Fortune tied in a chain, he usurps the power of God; in human terms he is arrogating that power which Pico della Mirandola saw as integral to the Dignity of Man. Instead of assigning man a place in the hierarchy of being, God confers on Adam the freedom of choice which enables him to transfer his degree of life from the highest to the lowest.

> Neither a fixed abode nor a form that is thine alone, nor any function peculiar to thyself have we given thee, Adam, to the end that according to thy judgment thou mayest have and possess what abode, what form, what functions thou thyself shalt desire. Constrained by no limits, in accordance with thine own free will, in whose hand we have placed thee, thou shalt ordain for thyself the limits of thy nature. Thou shalt have power to degenerate into the lower forms of life, which are brutish. Thou shalt have the power, out of thy soul's judgment, to be reborn into the higher forms which are divine.
>
> (Pico, *De Hominis Dignitate*, tr. in E. Cassirer, *The Renaissance Philosophy of Man*, pp. 224-5)

In Ralegh's *History of the World*, 'Man is described under the fable of Proteus, who was said as often as he pleased to change his shape'; the Protean form of Man was naturally manifest in the Protean art of the actor with peculiar force.

The medieval idea of Fortune satisfied Christian stoicism, for her action was a sublunary one, her seeming instability part of a hidden purpose which proceeded (though inscrutably) from the Providence of God; the proper response was one of resignation, of steadfastness in adversity and distrust of good Fortune. The attitude depends on the ontological separation of the realms of Time, where Fortune rules, and of Eternity where she has no part. Fortune's bright face, like the sun's, is sometimes clouded or sets. Dark Fortune was shewn with an evil visage; the Goddess was shewn sometimes as a monster with 'two faces under one hood,' sometimes as two sisters conjoined together.

Gradually Fortune became a more mutable image, no longer predominantly tragic, and in Shakespeare, though she appears everywhere in his poetry it is necessary to see how she is used in *this* poem, *this* play. She becomes a means of delineating experience rather than of ordering it. The ancient image no longer stands behind the usage.

For example, Shakespeare took *Romeo and Juliet* from a poem in which long laments against Fortune were based on Chaucer's *Troilus*, but he cuts all this to the single exclamation of Romeo when Tybalt is slain and he realizes the implications of this act; 'O, I am Fortune's fool!' Fortune none the less remains a key word in Shakespeare— it occupies four columns of print in the Concordance. In the comedies she is apt to be mocked, and she is often taken as Erasmus and Thomas More took her, as the patron of fools. The old formal image of the goddess is reduced to absurdity by the invocation of Ancient Pistol and the solemn pedantries of Fluellen:

> By your patience, Auncient Pistol, Fortune is painted plind, with a muffler afore her eyes, to signify unto you, that Fortune is plind; and she is painted also with a wheel to signify unto you that see, which is the moral of it, that she is turning and inconstant and mutability, and variation; and her foot, look you, is fixed upon a spherical stone which rolls and rolls and rolls; in good Truth, the poet makes a most excellent description of it; Fortune is an excellent moral. *(Henry V, 3.6.31-40)*

But hardly, after this, one available for the tragic dramatist; and Shakespeare was already more prone to the neutral term 'Fortunes'—as in the *Merchant of Venice*. In general, the good wits treat Fortune cavalierly and only the pompous characters take her seriously.

The disappearance of what had provided the main motive system for earlier tragedy left something of a vacuum; in *Julius Caesar* there remain the omens which suggest man's life is controlled by larger powers. Conflict with blind chance sends Cinna the poet out into the street in spite of his bad dream, to be torn to pieces by a mob because his name is Cinna The storm before Caesar's death—the omens before Philippi—suggest one interpretation of events, while such actions as Brutus' error over Antony's funeral or Cassius' error over the supposed capture of Titinius decisively change the course of the action. When a situation is already inescapable by means of human choice, omens indicate a sympathetic response from Nature, a sensitive reaction in the microcosm, more like an Early Warning System than a Messenger of Heavenly Wrath.

Hamlet and his fellow students mock Fortune as a strumpet, whose buffets or rewards are best ignored. Horatio, 'more an antique Roman than a Dane', claims the right so freely exercised by the Romans in *Julius Caesar*, and proudly proclaimed by the Epicurean and sceptical Cassius near the beginning:

> I know where I will wear this dagger then,
> Cassius from bondage shall deliver Cassius.
> Therein, ye Gods, ye make the weak most strong,
> Therein, ye Gods, ye tyrants do defeat.
> Nor stony towers nor walls of beaten brass,
> Nor airless dungeon, nor strong links of iron
> Can be retentive to the strength of spirit;
> But life, being weary of these worldly bars,
> Never lacks power to dismiss itself.
> If I know this, know all the world beside,
> That part of tyranny which I do bear
> I can shake off at leisure.   (1.3.89-100)

To which, rather deflating the grandeur, Casca the cowardly retorts:

> So can I;
> So every bondman in his own hand bears
> The hand to cancel his captivity.   (1.3.100-3)

This directly affronts the Christian view (as for instance it is given in military terms by Spenser's Red Cross Knight to Despair, *Faerie Queene*, I.x.xli)

> The term of life is limited:
> Ne may a man prolong or shorten it:
> The soldier may not move from watchful sted,
> Nor leave his stand until his Captain bed.
> Who life did limit by almighty doom
> (Quoth he) knows best the terms established:
> And he that points the Centinel his room
> Doth licence him depart at sound of morning drum.

and indeed it affronts the stoic view that man proves his superiority to the gods by enduring the worst that can befall. Just before the last battle Brutus stoically condemns Cato's doctrine of suicide, yet he accepts this end for himself and his friends (only the young Cato, Portia's brother is killed in battle). The others take what is considered the soldierly and honourable way of avoiding capture and triumph, and thereby earn a soldier's burial rites. This is less a contravention of Brutus' principle than the final act of the battle itself, the noblest and most self-affirming way of conceding victory.

> By your leave, Gods, is a Roman's part.
> Come, Cassius' sword and find Titinius' heart.

At the opening, Brutus had said:

> Set honour in one eye and death i' the other,
> And I will look on both indifferently   (1.2.85-6)

and throughout the play offers of voluntary death fall thick and fast. Caesar offers the populace his throat (perhaps it is only the kind of wooing device which makes Richard offer his sword to Lady Anne); Cassius offers his throat to Brutus in the quarrel scene; Antony offers himself to the conspirators to be cut off with Caesar, and Brutus tells the people he has a dagger ready for himself whenever it shall please his country to need his death.

Such suicide is close to ritual sacrifice, as it is presented in Marston's *Sophonisba*, or Webster's *Appius and Virginia*, where women are sacrificed to preserve their chastity by their nearest and dearest; and in the latter case, the murderer dies also by his own hand.

The divine kings of Africa, as Monica Wilson has reminded us not so long ago, are sacrificed when their vitality is diminished. These divine kings lose their divine stature and become ordinary mortal kings when they cease to be symbols of unity and acquire secular power: foreign trade in ivory and cloth transformed the divine king into a magistrate who acquired a government court.[7]

Titinius dies on Cassius' sword, for friendship's sake, Brutus in an attempt to appease the daimon that had haunted him. His act is the expiation of one who had been 'Caesar's angel'; it is the reply to 'et tu, Brute?'

> Caesar, now be still,
> I kill'd not thee with half so good a will.
>
> (5.5.50-1)

He had known that this day 'must end the work the Ides of March began'; yet even at the end he affirms friendship for the inescapable hypnotic attraction of his fatally naive idealism has never deserted him.

> Countrymen,
> My heart doth joy that yet in all my life,
> I found no man but he was true to me.
>
> (5.5.33-5)

Caesar, of course, was not so fortunate.

E. M. Forster said if he had to choose between betraying his friend and betraying his country he hoped he would have the guts to betray his country. Brutus attempts to appease his loyalty by seeing the act as a religious sacrifice.

> Let us be sacrificers but not butchers. . . .
> Let's carve him as a dish fit for the gods.
>
> (2.1.166-73)

The ritual nature of the act is emphasized by the ceremony of washing in Caesar's blood, with the portentous reflections of a sacrament.

> How many ages hence,
> Shall this our lofty scene be acted o'er
> In states unborn and actions yet unknown!
>
> (3.1.111-13)

But to Antony it *is* simply an act of butchery; and butchers is what he calls them. The two speeches in the market place are an extension of this double judgment. Caesar had been permitted a formal funeral, with full rites, but Antony, with no sense of the portentous at all, seizes the occasion and the microphone, acts Brutus off the lofty stage, lets loose the dogs of war upon all Italy, and meets the ceremonial violence of the assassination with a greater natural violence that was probably, for Shakespeare and his audience the ultimate worst thing—an enraged City mob.

Antony says the conspirators' daggers hacked one another in the sides of Caesar as they hewed him as a carcase fit for hounds; below Pompey's statue the colossus of the world sank a mere bleeding piece of earth. His wounds, horridly described as dumb mouths, turn this hunted animal into a hunter; then he in turn becomes the random slayer.

> With Ate by his side come hot from hell.

The ritual sacrifice was to be so efficacious that no programme is needed: nothing was planned to succeed, for the conspirators expect Rome to right itself if Caesar is removed. Antony's conspiracy is better than artifice for he is relying on the instability of political life, and on diplomacy as the art of the possible. A sceptical attitude towards all ceremony is endorsed by the sophistication of Antony's political technique. Antony and Octavius know that guilt is inseparable from power, that power exists to be used.

Caesar's remark which Ben Jonson scoffed at till Shakespeare removed it, 'Caesar did never wrong but with just cause', was too sophisticated a paradox for most Elizabethans to accept; yet 'conscious acceptance of guilt in the necessary murder', which the conspirators try to evade, is assumed by the triumvirate in their bloody proscription with no debate at all.

The almost irresistible temptation to make a thesis or a debate of the issue does not even arise, for in this play debate occurs within the mind of Caesar (between his natural fears and his public image) and of Brutus. A natural solitary, in the orchard under the blazing light of the great storm or in the tent with the single candle, Brutus takes his lonely and fatally mistaken decisions. As a politician he is inflexible, unadaptable, since, having with such difficulty conquered his scruples, he is then unable to deviate; the pride of his descent from the original tyrant queller, with more than a trace of patrician hauteur and reticence, dominate the conspirators, but the qualities that make him so valuable as a figurehead create only a momentary effect on the Roman crowd. As Cassius succeeds in tempting Brutus, so Antony, in a technique that foreshadows the methods of that other 'honest man', Iago, suggests and implants feelings which he simultaneously (in his overt statements) forbids, and thereby raises them to a higher pitch.

The play is not about Caesar or Cassius or Brutus; it is about the high and palmy state of Rome. The opening scene shews the dignity of the *polis*; statues are decorated with garlands and citizens come in their holiday attire. To the Londoners it would recall a coronation day, or some other triumphal entry. By the assassination, all power is put in balance; and till the balance is restored, power reverts to the people, who are Caesar's heirs in a deeper sense than the testamentary one. The complete anarchy of firing the conspirators' houses—an act which imperils the whole city —is a terrifying demonstration of the volcanic forces that boil below the thin crust of order. Shakespeare had shewn the mob taking over London in *Henry VI* and in the Ill May Day sequence of *Sir Thomas More;* here the crowd of decent artisans, cobblers and market men murder the poet. It is essentially an Elizabethan mob.

Two forms of social disorder combine in this play—the dangerous cross currents of great affairs, where great men learnt to manipulate situations by double bluff, skilful use of a cat's-paw; also by exploiting a second great source of disorder—the instability and sudden fury of the *plebeians*. To present such disorder is to recover the sense of the past in its contingency, the 'openness' of situations as they were before history decided the outcome.

This recovery of the past, as it felt when it happened, was possible only when the deep traces of the older sacramental view, and the images which carried it far below the level of conscious thought, had been dissolved by interplay between actor and actor, actor and audience. The autonomy of the present moment is written into this play by the quality of its rhetorical poetry.

The drama of the theatre, of the market place, and of the study culminates in the joy that Brutus encounters in the dust of defeat, with the sleep that so long evaded him:

> Night hangs upon mine eyes; my bones would rest
> That have but laboured to attain this hour. (5.5.141-3)

Shakespeare's contemporaries were more impressed by the quarrel between Brutus and Cassius than by the assassination or forum scenes. A friend says that this 'Half-sword parley' 'ravished the audience' who went 'wondering thence'. It 'took nobly'—that is, it charmed the spectators by contrast with Ben Jonson's classical tragedies:

> they would not brook a line
> Of tedius, though well-labour'd *Catiline*;
> *Sejanus* too was irksome.
> (Leonard Digges, *Lines* prefixed to Poems of 1640)

Up to the quarrel, Roman gravitas and constancy had partly compensated for that older set of images which tragedy had supplied. But here is a second break-through —the strained, pointless wrangle of two overwrought men, no longer patrician or stoic but suddenly childish, rebuked by the absurd poet. The scene has all the arbitrary quality, all the depth and nature that Brutus' rituals lacked, and brings them to the certitude in uncertainty of their farewell. Action has swept beyond them; the tide in the affairs of men, which once brought Cassius to save Caesar's life in the Tiber (a story of Shakespeare's invention) is to drive them to a stormy ocean.

> Why now, blow wind, swell billow and swim bark!
> The storm is up, and all is on the hazard.   (5.1.67-8)

In *Julius Caesar* the omens on the eve of Caesar's murder, and before the battle of Philippi may suggest an organic link between Man and Nature, but the free decisions, the regretted mistakes, the contradiction of 'hateful Error, Melancholy's child' counterbalance this suggestion. The contradiction is not resolved. Similarly, the stern limitation upon conduct imposed by the stoic code, and by Roman tradition, the absence of feminine indecision, except in the minor figure of Portia, suggest a massive and heroic series of public acts, which the tide of events could not modify, yet this again is contradicted. The arts of power, as Shakespeare depicts them, turn the funeral scene into a public trial.

In the year 1599, what basis had Shakespeare for such a view of history? In his own career, his fellowship had just passed through a crisis, from which it had emerged much strengthened in unity and security, after a rather lawless act of self help. He wrote a play in which general relations of a group of men supplies the main conflict system. In government, it must have been felt that England was facing a power vacuum. The Queen at sixty-six was inevitably nearing the end of her reign; the Earl of Essex, to whom men looked, returned in disgrace from Ireland in September 1599 and was living from court, but had not yet committed that final act of folly by which he tried (8 February, 1601) to raise the City of London against the Crown, and for which, before the month was out, he suffered execution. Unease, discouragement and above all suspense and tension must have been the mood. The Earl of Southampton, who had been in Ireland with Essex and returned with him, in the autumn months of 1599 lived at Essex House with the Earl of Rutland and 'they pass the time in London merely in going to plays every day'.[8] So they were likely to have seen the early performances of *Julius Caesar*.

Chapman, no theatrical expert, felt that enactment 'by the personal and exact life it gives to any history or other such delineation of human actions, adds to them lustre, apprehension and spirit' (dedication to *Caesar and Pompey*).

The decade following *Julius Caesar* witnessed a great number of political tragedies by Marston and Webster, Jonson and Chapman; the last at particular length defended suicide.[9] The self conqueror, Cato, was substituted for a Tamburlaine—he who preferred defeat. Shakespeare returned to the Lives of the Noble Romans only at the end of the decade with *Coriolanus* and *Antony and Cleopatra*, round 1608-9.

Here the balancing of pros and cons in the political situation is radically sceptical. *Coriolanus* is a City Tragedy whose hero, shewing man at his most arrogant, and secretly perhaps at his most desperate, maintains his inflexible nobility at the price of inflammable rage. The rage is the price paid for the nobility; the tragedy of his private relationships issues in the tragedy of his public relationships, which interact at every level. His mother wins him by the means that the others use to undo him, his inability to resist a taunt. Yet banishment from the City walls leaves Coriolanus, in spite of his trite stoic maxims, unable to find any reason why life should continue. At the centre of this play are two great gaps in statement—the gap where he decides to join the Volsces, and the moment when he stands with his mother and (it is Shakespeare's direction) 'holds her by the hand silent' before accepting the plea that is, as he well knows, 'most mortal to him'. A double warfare rages in this play, the war without Rome and the war within; in spite of Menenius' fable of the belly, the love and hate felt in this group are those of the kindred, of the small group who exist only in relation to each other, but whose aims were in fact divided. In this packed urban society the great man stands lonely and takes even adulation as cruelty in the end. The ladies, finally entering through the cheering Roman mob to the noise of every instrument the Shakespearean theatre could muster, frozen figures of grief in their mourning garments, are as alien to the rejoicing as Coriolanus entering the enemy city to drums, trumpets and shouting of the mob that will shortly be yelling for his blood.

Though he finds 'I melt, and am not of stronger earth than others', Coriolanus attempts to live as a god among men—the incarnation of Mars. 'Now the great goddess Fortune fall deep in love with thee' is the prayer of his general Cominius; but the fickle crowd embody both his Fortune and his Fate. The play is deeply ambiguous; both right- and left-wing politicians have utilized it, the most notable adaptation being Brecht's.

In *Antony and Cleopatra*, although Antony is descended from the god Hercules, and Cleopatra is the incarnation of Isis, mutability rules. We have left the *polis* and the little world of Rome for the whole Mediterranean world, and there is room neither for the high argument of *Julius Caesar* nor the rigid codes of *Coriolanus*. Fortune rules— the very word occurs again and again; and for Antony the good and evil aspects of his Fortune are embodied in Octavia and Cleopatra; they correspond to what is divided in Antony himself, the Roman captain and the lover of the Royal Egypt. In Rome 'he married but his Occasion'. The 'great fairy', queen and gipsy, herself mutable yet from that drawing strength, at Antony's death rails against the 'false huswife Fortune' and sets up her decision to shackle accident and bolt up change.

> My desolation does begin to make
> A better life. 'Tis paltry to be Caesar;
> Not being Fortune, he's but Fortune's knave,
> A minister of her will.   (5.2.1-4)

Here, it may be thought, is the return in transmuted form of the magic of royalty. Cleopatra the tawny gipsy, 'with Phoebus' amorous pinches black' may recall not only the

'Infinite variety' of Protean humanity but a specific stage occasion of great symbolic significance in the relations between the Crown and the Stage.

An African Queen, richly robed in pearl and blue and silver had floated on the Whitehall stage in January 1605, for Ben Jonson's Twelfth Night Masque, when the Twelve Daughters of Niger (which some called the Nile), led by Anne of Denmark, appeared in a sea shell riding towards the spectators.

What Jacobean could fail to remember the first royal performance by a Queen of England? The extraordinary effect of seeing her also disguised as a negress would have marked this masque for the contemporaries. It stands as a landmark also (as has been shewn by Glynne Wickham) dividing the old form of stage and the new, with its new perspective scenery and proscenium arch.[10] 'From *The Masque of Blackness* we can look forward over the next three centuries.'

Spectacular glories which could not be scenically rivalled by Shakespeare were poetically challenged—we may be sure he would have moved heaven and earth to see his rival's great triumph, and as one of the King's Men he would probably have been called for duty.

Seen in contemporary terms you might say, here is an ancient, deeply traditional, deeply personal form of royal government, absolutist but disorganized and doomed, the household rule of regal pomp and personal influence, of bounty that is wasteful, of fidelity that can last to death. Confronting it is a strict, regulated, even more absolutist form of government, which works through council and planning, strategy rather than force of arms, the skilful and patient following of self-interest. The household form of government and the bureaucratic form of government had been at issue with each other throughout the Tudor century as Professor Geoffrey Elton has so amply shewn; but the conflict for Shakespeare was also within himself. He lived like one of the new men, amassing a prudent fortune, yet he chose to live and die in the little town where he had been born.

In *Antony and Cleopatra*, not only has man regained
something of his godlike stature, not only is fickle Fortune
embodied in the moods of a gipsy, but there is a new sense
of theatrical pageantry and triumph. No longer fixed and
secure, but shadowy and evanescent, the pageantry of a
dream, a masque simultaneously enlarges and reduces the
stature of godlike beings, Protean representatives of Pico
della Mirandola's divine man.

> Sometimes we see a cloud that's dragonish,
> A vapour sometimes like a bear or lion,
> A tower'd citadel, a pendent rock,
> A forked mountain or blue promontory,
> With trees upon't that nod into the world
> And mock our eyes with air; thou hast seen these signs.
> They are black vesper's pageants. Even with a thought
> The rack dislimns, and makes it indistinct,
> As water is in water.
> My good knave Eros, now thy captain is
> Even such a body; here I am Antony,
> Yet cannot hold this visible shape, my knave. (4.14.2-14)

In this magnificent stormy sunset there is conveyed without
full unfolding the imaginative form of this play. No history,
belonging with the shew of *Timon of Athens*, it is a play that
begins within one dimension, containing large elements of
satire, to end within another, in a lyric affirmation upon a
cosmic scene.

A succession of baroque pageants proceeds from the
Bacchanals on Pompey's ship, followed immediately by the
noble Roman tableau of Ventidius 'as it were in triumph,
the dead body of Pacorus born before him'; Octavia enters
between Antony and Caesar; the subterranean music leads
the soldiers bewilderedly following it; Enobarbus laments
beneath the glimpses of the moon. In Plutarch, Antony is
masquer and reveller and the language of Plutarch links
him with common players. Cleopatra mocks:

> Good now, play me one scene
> Of excellent dissembling—let it look
> Like perfect honour.   (1.3.78-80)

Together they roam the streets in disguise; she drinks him to bed, puts her tires on him and wears his Philippian sword. Their play is doomed to end in a Roman triumph, with the quick comedians extemporizing upon the theme of their love. But throughout, the lovers have been devising rôles for one another to play, and each imagining the other in contradictory styles; Antony is at once a Gorgon and a Mars.

After Antony's death, Cleopatra recounts her dream of him to the puzzled Dolabella, an Antony 'past the size of dreaming' yet one who is 'Nature's piece 'gainst fancy, contemning shadows quite'. A gorgeous cosmic figure, as of some great pageant, he imprints upon the whole cosmos the form of Man, a giant such as those Goya depicts in the Prado in his Peintures Noires.

> I dreamed there was an Emperor Antony . . .
> O such another sleep, that I might see
> But such another man!
> His face was as the heavens, and therein stuck
> A sun and moon, which kept their course and lightened
> This little O, the earth.
> His legs bestrid the ocean, his rear'd arm
> Crested the world; his voice was propertied
> As all the tuned spheres, and that to friends,
> But when he meant to quail and shake the orb,
> It was as rattling thunder. For his bounty,
> There was no winter in't; and autumn 'twas,
> That grew the more by reaping. . . .   (5.2.75-100)

When in the opening scene, Cleopatra says 'I'll set a bourne how far to be beloved', Antony replies 'Then must thou needst find out new heavens, new earth'. This new earth and heaven is denied by Dolabella:

> Think you there was, or might be, such a man
> As this I dreamt of?
> Gentle madam, no.

The destruction of Antony is sharply and ruthlessly given in Roman terms—not only by his enemy Caesar but his friend Enobarbus, whose ironic comments puncture

THE LIVES OF THE NOBLE ROMANS

the inflated grandeur of the Egyptian scenes. Yet they do not destroy it; and it is Enobarbus who described the goddess Cleopatra—Isis sailing down the river of Cydnus. There is no blurring of incompatibles. Octavia is but Occasion ('he married but his Occasion here'), Cleopatra but a spectacle like the pyramids. 'Would I had never seen her,' exclaims Antony, to which Enobarbus replies:

> O, sir, you have then left unseen a wonderful piece of work, which not to have been blessed withal would have discredited your travel.   (1.2.153-6)

What then is offered? Joseph Conrad supplies one possible answer to these lives of the Noble Romans, with their stoic ethics and their irrational self-wrecking.

> The ethical view of the universe involves us at last in so many cruel and absurd contradictions, where the last vestiges of faith, hope and charity, and even of reason itself are ready to perish that I have come to suspect the aim of creation cannot be ethical at all. . . . Those visions . . . are a moral end in themselves. The rest is our affair—the laughter, the tears, the tenderness, the indignation, the high tranquillity of a steeled heart, the detached curiosity of a subtle mind—that's our affair!
>
> (*A Personal Record, Collected Works*, 1923, p. 92)

CHAPTER VII

OLD THINGS MADE NEW:
HAMLET, PRINCE OF DENMARK

i. The Older 'Hamlet' Plays

SHAKESPEARE'S *Hamlet* is the culmination of a line of plays, now either lost or long forgotten. Thomas Kyd's *Hamlet* was followed after a decade by a group of bravura shew-pieces for boys, to which Shakespeare replied with a drama that ever since has continuously challenged fresh experiments for which it forms the basis. *Hamlet* is not so much a play as a geological deposit of accumulated dramatic experience. It *is* the embodied history of the English stage—this because of the intensity of its demands upon successive generations, calling out all they can give, more than they knew they had to give. Because it is most traditional in theme, it is most revolutionary in terms of relationships, their precision, their definition by gestures married to words.

Sartre said, in *Qu'est que c'est que la littérature?*

> Tintoretto did not choose that yellow rift in the sky above Golgotha to *signify* anguish, or to *provoke* it. It is anguish and yellow sky at the same time. Not sky of anguish or anguished sky; it is anguish become thing, anguish which has turned into a yellow rift of sky, and which is thereby submerged and impasted by the proper quality of things, by their impermeability, their extension, and that infinity of relations which they maintain with other things. . . . The empire of signs is prose; poetry is on the side of painting, sculpture and music. For the poet, language is a structure of the external world.

For the poetic dramatist, this structure is reinforced by the living stage.

When in the second scene of *Hamlet* we reach that point where Claudius turns to the silent figure in black:

But now, my cousin Hamlet, and my son—
HAM. A little more than kin and less than kind.
CLA. How is it that the clouds still hang on you?
HAM. Not so, my lord; I am too much i' the sun.

(1.2.64-7)

then we hear the voice of one who is 'condemned to be an
individual'—yet also a voice in which much dramatic
experience is distilled—a pun from the opening line of
Richard III, the bastard Falconbridge's breaking of decorum, and the undertones of the lost play by Kyd, with
its atmospheric intensities, which Shakespeare used as a
launching platform for his dazzling ascent. Hamlet the
prince embodies anguish as does the yellow rift of sky;
the play 'represents an enormous effort to move forward
to the heroism of the individual without abandoning
the older social and religious framework of external
action'.[1]

As *Julius Caesar* represents advance by Innovation,
Hamlet stands for Reformation. The key word of the older
lost play, we know, was the shriek of 'the ghost that cried
so miserably at the Theatre like an oyster wife, Hamlet
Revenge!' From the little *Hystorie of Hamblet* preserved
at Trinity College, the 'book of the play', we learn the key
word of Shakespeare's version—Hamlet's triumphant jest
'A rat, a rat!' as he plunged his sword into the arras and
killed Polonius.

A glimpse of the atmospheric qualities and cosmic
setting of the lost play is afforded by the Induction which
survives with a debased acting version of *Hamlet* preserved
in German; for this Induction is clearly far more authentic
and archaic than the play, and requires, physically, the old
emblematic stage of the Elizabethans, a three-storied
universe, in which dark powers from above and below
unite against Man.

Night or Hecate descends from the heavens in her car,
saying:

Before Phoebus shine, I will begin a game.
Up, Furies, up, and shew yourselves.

Rising to meet her as she descends, the Furies ask her commands. Night, poppy-crowned, friend and light of incendiaries, declares she will throw her mantle over the adulterous pair, while the Furies, working within the human breast, sow dissension, poison the marriage bed, kindle a fire of revenge and let the sparks fly over the realm. In turn the Furies promise to exceed her wishes and Alecto concludes:

> I fan the sparks and make the fire burn:
> Ere it dawn the second time, the whole game I'll shew.

Night ascends in her chariot, while the furies sink.[2]

This emblem for a rite or 'game' of death provides for such a framework as the Ghost of Andrea and Revenge in Kyd's surviving play, *The Spanish Tragedy*. The whole action is predetermined and fixed by that special kind of language which is revived in Shakespeare's *Hamlet*, for use by the Murderer in the play within the play:

> Thoughts black, hands apt, drugs fit and time agreeing,
> Confederate season, else no creature seeing,
> Thou mixture rank, of midnight weed collected,
> By Hecate's ban thrice blasted, thrice infected,
> Thy natural magic and dire property
> On wholesome life usurp immediately.   (3.2.270-5)

Hamlet himself prompts this murderer to begin by wildly misquoting lines from the early version of *Richard III*:

> Begin murderer, pox, leave thy damnable faces and begin.
> Come:
> 'The croaking raven doth bellow for revenge' (3.2.268-9)

Yet a little later, after the recorders' scene, Hamlet himself speaks like a ventriloquist, with the voice of the older character, in a sympathetic response to the contagious effect of the 'confederate season', preparing for his decision *not* to kill the king at prayers.

> 'Tis now the very witching time of night,
> That churchyards yawn, and hell itself breathes out
> Contagion to the world; now could I drink hot blood

And do such bitter business as the day
Would quake to look on. (3.2.413-7)

Lucianus, nephew to the King, speaks here, opening per-
spectives upon different dramatic levels already established.
The lines present a serious problem for the modern actor,
who cannot rely on audience-memory of older Revenge
Plays.

Revenge, a lust of the blood and a permission of the will,
is, as Bacon said, a kind of wild justice, which the more
man's nature runs to, the more ought law to root it out.
But if the fountain-head of justice is poisoned, the dark
road upon the left hand side may be the only one,[3] even if it
lead to hell. 'Terror is the feeling which arrests the mind in
the presence of whatever is grave and constant in human
suffering and unites it with the hidden cause.'[4]

The agonising dilemma of the Old Revenge Dramas
was that of Law negated (Elizabethans thought of tragedy
in terms of great public action) combined with Love and
Self-Love negated; a complex double stress gives great
strength to the native form, evolved by the good craftsman
Thomas Kyd from schoolboy Latin—but Ovid rather than
Seneca.[5]

By the early 1590s a firm convention of imagery—
blood, night and furies, the reflexion of an eschatology of
Death, Hell and Judgment—was joined to a firm convention of action and characters, the skeleton of the revenge
plot. An unrelieved tension was lightened only by ironic
reversals, mockery and derision; consistency of impression, maintained by a common idiom, gave to the actors a
framework within which they could block out effects and
develop their own technique. It was at once a support to
them and an open invitation. The Revenge play belongs
essentially to the professional repertory stage; the first
creator of Kyd's rôles was Edward Alleyn.

Of Jeronymo, the Judge turned avenger, hero of *The
Spanish Tragedy* it is said:

On his shoulders comes the burden of the world's justice . . .
in the closing disaster, there is a kind of triumph, but no one

feels it except the dead man who has been watching from the shadows ... Kyd left a blank where the moral dramatist would have set a seal of Christian approval or of disapproval or his presumptuous indication of the hand of heaven. And he has therefore written a tragedy and not a tract.

(Philip Edwards, *Thomas Kyd*, 1966, pp. 39-40)

Events interlock completely in the close-wrought impermeability of this play; the word 'mercy' does not occur. At the climax, a play within the play shews that 'we die in earnest, that's no jest'—and the final dumb shew reveals and unites the hero with the 'hidden cause', the body of his murdered son, now so amply revenged.

The craft model of Kyd—a black plot of strident ghosts, a man waked from sleep to living nightmare, driven by the denial of justice to play a double part—was adapted by Shakespeare in *Titus Andronicus;* and in Peter Brook's production of this play, modern audiences were given some sense of the power of these earlier Revenge plays, precursors of *Hamlet*. A pageant of Menace—according to Armin, 'There are, as Hamlet says, things called whips'[6]—gradually narrows down to an interior conflict. In the final silence of outrage, Jeronymo bites out his own tongue, as Richard III 'finds in myself no pity to myself'. Human flesh—or animal flesh—turns against itself in the last Thyestean astonishments of *Titus Andronicus*, ravening and devouring.

This kind of black drama continued alongside the new craft forms. In 1625, John Milton, rusticated from Cambridge, spent his time going to the Theatre, and seems to have enjoyed primitive horrors, which he describes to Diodati as 'raving Tragedy shaking a blood-stained sceptre with the cruel Avenger recrossing the Styx to terrify the guilty with the glare of his funeral brand'.[7]

ii. The New Revenge Plays

Perhaps a decade after it was written, *The Spanish Tragedy* received its revision, the confrontation of Jeronymo with the old Painter seeking from him the justice he cannot get for himself. Jeronymo in his sore distraction asks the man not for a spatial design of the original murder, but a temporal composition—a *drama*, 'impasted by the quality of things' that will not cease to haunt him.

> Can'st paint me a tear or a wound, a groan or a sigh? . . . Let the clouds scowl, make the moon dark, the stars extinct, the winds blowing, the bells tolling, the owl shrieking, the toads croaking, the minutes jarring, and the clock striking twelve. And then at last, sir, starting, behold a man hanging and tottering, as you know the wind will weave a man, and with a trice to cut him down. And looking upon him by the advantage of my torch, find it to be my son Horatio. There you may shew a passion, there you may shew a passion. Draw me like old Priam of Troy, crying, The House is afire, the house is afire, as the torch over my head
> (Additions, Fourth Addition, 113-4. 147-58)

Here is 'the motive and the cue for passion' in the theatre itself. But the new creation of scenes from within by the actor's 'passion' was subject to parody.

The little singing boys of St Paul's gave a painter's scene to the fool in *Antonio and Mellida*, their new comedy of the absurd:

> Can you paint me a drivelling reeling song and let the word be Ugh?   (5.1.27-8)

Yet the second part of their two-part shew (by the youthful John Marston) offered the first of the new Revenge Plays, where tragic term mingled with the absurd. Variety now replaced consistency; ritual was balanced by improvisation; bitter comedy was grafted on to the old ironic drama. There was continuity, in distinction to the sharp break between the old and new type of history play. The action of *Antonio's Revenge*, put on before 1600, summarized in the words of its ghost, is a twin to the action of *Hamlet*.

> Antonio, Revenge!
> Thy mother yields consent
> To be his wife, and give his blood a son
> That made her husbandless and doth complot
> To make her sonless.   (3.1.34ff.)

The choristers offered a virtuoso's performance, full of
operatic contrast in various passions. The narrative exists
in token outline only. Extreme violence is both indulged
and satirized in a series of histrionic displays, each actor
giving solo arias in turn. Marston's 'satiric art feeds on
rejection, including the ground on which the rejector himself stood'.[8] The medley of passion, artifice, mockery makes
no attempt at consistency; there is no plot, only a final rush:
'Vengeance, to't, pell mell!' In a Black Requiem rite,
Antonio kills the usurper's child, and sprinkles the blood
on the tomb of his own murdered parent: the sentiments
would fit with the prologue of the Old *Hamlet*.

> And now, swart night, to swell thy hour out,
> Behold I spurt warm blood in thy black eyes.
>
> (3.1.193-4)

while the language is directly violent in a new way, representing the inflamed feeling that on another occasion,
makes Antonio envy the placidity of the fool.

> Had heaven been kind
> Creating me an honest senseless dolt,
> A good poor fool, I should want sense to feel
> The stings of anguish shoot through every vein . . .
> I should not thus run mad
> As one confounded in a maze of mischief. . . .
>
> (4.1.49-52, 55-6)

And so he puts on the motley and appears in the garb and
habit of a fool, blowing soap bubbles in the Court where
his beloved is on trial for her life:

> Puff, hold world; puff, hold bubble; puff, hold world.
>
> (4.1.99)

The successive betrayals which are the only principle of
structure throughout both parts of this play mean that one
attitude is constantly collapsing to reveal the unexpected
co-existence of another; while in the Induction, the little
actors come on to discuss their parts. In advance, therefore
they are mocking and undermining their own performance.

By the next season a new troupe of boys had started up in Burbage's Blackfriars Theatre, and according to the early actors' version of Shakespeare's *Hamlet*:

> The principal public audience that
> Came to them [i.e. the men] are turn'd to private plays
> And to the humours of children.   (Q.1, 2.2.353-5)

So Rosencrantz can smile, thinking there will be no welcome for the players who are on the road after their discomfiture; the boys carry it away, he tells Hamlet, 'Hercules and his load too'. Hercules bearing the Globe was the sign of the men's playhouse.

The arrival of the Players at Elsinore could not really have been staged at the Globe except as part of a dazzling public success. No one really advertises his own failure. But this scene, actually staged at the Globe, shews the players trudging away from it. Immediately after the handsome advertisement by Polonius (... 'for the law of writ and liberty, these are the only men' should be read from a scroll, I think), 'Enter the players'. The first player naturally is Burbage, and he confronts the real Burbage (who is of course playing Hamlet) made up with the small pointed beard familiar from the Dulwich portrait. 'What!' asks the original, commenting on the unexpected addition to his understudy's countenance, 'thy face is valenced since I saw thee last; com'st thou to beard me in Denmark?' Shakespeare had long been haunted by the idea of the double self in the twins of his comedies, the rival queens of his tragic stories competing for one identity. This should be remembered throughout the performance which follows, and Burbage's soliloquy.

> O what a rogue and peasant slave am I!
> Is it not monstrous that this player here,
> But in a fiction, in a dream of passion
> Could force his soul so to his own conceit
> That from her working all his visage wan'd . . . .
>   (2.2.584-8)

For Burbage was particularly celebrated himself for doing just that.[9]

Dick Burbage met his double reciting some lines about the Fall of Troy which are caviare to the general. Later, Burbage as Hamlet jests with Polonius about the two last parts they had played, with a pun which perhaps had been used as a playhouse jest; to the old man who claims to have been killed as Julius Caesar in the Capitol, the actor of Brutus replies: 'It was a brute part of him to kill so capital a calf there!' The point of the exchange depends on the identity of the actors.

But here is no children's variety shew. It is 'the fury and the mire of human veins'. There *was* variety in the part—Dr Johnson termed it the characteristic virtue of the play; and the rôle was played in Restoration times as that of a youth, 'a young man of great expectation, vivacity and enterprise'.[10]

A real exertion of power was called for to teach the boys their place, but not only in the leading rôle: 'from the myopic shrewdness of Polonius to the troubled but profound intuitions of Ophelia', Shakespeare's great range of style calls for variety from all the cast. Open bantering of the children and of part of the audience is carried a stage further before long, and the self-conscious confrontation of actor with himself becomes a very familiar jest; further twists are given to the new revenge convention.

Some two or three years after Shakespeare's *Hamlet*, the King's Men, as his company then was, acquired by some rather uncertain means Marston's *The Malcontent* from the Blackfriars boys, and put it on with an Induction, which opens as follows:

Enter Will Sly, a tireman following him with a stool.
TIREMAN. Sir, the gentlemen will be angry if you sit here.
SLY. Why? we may sit upon the stage at the private house; thou dost not take me for a country gentleman, dost? dost, think I fear hissing? I'll hold my life thou took'st me for one of the players.
TIREMAN. No, sir.
SLY. . . . Where's Harry Condell, Dick Burbage and Will Sly? let me speak with some of them.

In their own persons, Burbage, Condell and Lowin then walk on, and the gallant after a line of Osric's part and Osric's business with his hat, charges them with producing a bitter play. Condell and Burbage defend it, and explain that because 'the book was lost' 'we found it and play it'— 'Why not Malevole in folio with us as Jeronimo in decimo sexto with them?' The players' revenge upon the boys provides them with a title (a well known way of passing off old plays!): '*We* call it One for Another'.

'Doth he play the Malcontent?' asks the gallant, as Burbage retires with 'I must leave you, sir'. 'Yes, sir,' answers Condell. Whereupon the challenge is issued: 'I dare lay four of my ears'—he must be wearing a fool's cap with ass's ears—'the play is not so well acted as it hath been'.

'O no, sir,' answers Condell ironically, 'nothing *ad Parmenonis suem.*'

Parmeno, according to Plutarch, could imitate the grunting of a pig so well that when a genuine pig competed with him, his admirers still cried 'Nothing to Parmeno's pig!'

What follows is a black comedy of revenge humours, but unlike Marston's earlier plays, it is fully articulated; the plot depends on the hero being throughout masked as a railing and villainous character. 'The mask, not the face is the emblem of this world'; only under a mask can goodness work to detect crime. This play belongs to an actors' theatre and exploits their conventions. 'A duke there is and the scene is Italy, as those things lightly we never miss' —but it is the Italy of competing power politics, of warring gangsters, Guicciardini's Italy. The author had an Italian mother; he knew at least the literature of the country.[11]

Themes of revenge, of black comedy, were bandied like tennis balls, in the 'War of the Theatres'; here is a kind of anti-play to Shakespeare's *Hamlet* for the King's Men. In this competitive situation, regrafted on an old stock, *Hamlet* rose like a rocket with three boosters, although the boosters have dropped into oblivion long ago. Yet we must not forget that at the time they added energy. We know that

Hamlet was popular enough to be pirated by the printers, that it also produced a whole crop of imitations, from the one we have just considered to Chettle's *Hoffman*, one of the worst plays ever scraped together, for which Henslowe paid its author a first intalment of 5s. on the 29 December, 1602. *Hoffman* would be given at the rival playhouse, The Fortune; and perhaps some of the jokes about the strumpet Fortune were barbed ones, implying that Alleyn's new theatre sign would suit a brothel.

In *The Malcontent* and its Induction, the audience is cajoled, mocked, parodied, but given a full assurance that nothing personal is intended; there are no Mousetrap lines here (Hamlet's court performance by the way has all the character of a *private* theatre, and he finds it necessary to warn the actors against putting in a gag or two against Polonius).

This play was published with an introduction that apologized for 'scenes merely invented to be spoken,' though it was admitted they had pleased many 'when presented with the soul of lively action'. It is plain that the Globe shared the questioning and satiric mood which the boys' theatre initiated; in the next decade, as Brian Gibbons notes in his book on City Comedy, 'the King's Men performed nearly every major play in the period, irrespective of its style'.

The range of Hamlet's part and of the other parts is more demanding than in any other of Shakespeare's plays. Consider the Ghost (one tradition gives the part to the author). For a long time he is silent, the effect being recorded by other players:

> It harrows me with fear and wonder

says the sceptical Horatio. Earlier ghosts were much more violent.

Hamlet himself may have acted very violently. *The Hystorie of Hamblet* speaks of him in the closet scene crowing like a cock and beating the air with his arms. When he decided to assume an antic disposition, he took on a player's part. An antic was a grotesque dumb player with an animal's head or an ugly mask; antics appear *only* in plays or dreams—they are not part of the everyday world.[12] After the extreme violence of the fight in the graveyard Hamlet turns on himself and Laertes with an ironic animal comparison:

> Let Hercules himself do what he may,
> The cat will mew and dog will have his day
>
> (5.1.313-4)

His sardonic wit often expresses itself in the rejection of familiar proverbs or in forcing an exchange of verbal weapons on his opponent: the double vision of madness allows a radical reshaping of the 'normal' ways of speech and perception and this is the creative and restorative aspect of mental disturbance.

> Conception is a blessing—but as your daughter may conceive— friend, look to't. (2.2.188-9)

> The Mousetrap. Marry how? tropically. (3.2.250)

'Marry trap' was the jeer used to a plotter whose own plot had recoiled on himself: when Silence threatens Nym with arrest, Nym snarls 'I will say marry trap with you if you run the nuthook's humour on me'.

The pageant of Polonius' death is concluded with a final farewell to his tediousness as the guts are lugged into the neighbouring room: 'Come sir, to draw towards an end with you'. The misapplication of names between his parents is a regular turn of Hamlet's wit.

> GER. Hamlet, thou hast thy father much offended.
> HAM. Mother, you have my father much offended.
>
> (3.4.9-10)

His refusal ever to call Claudius father[13] is justified by the final treachery of the King's smiling boast to Gertrude in the duel scene, 'Our son shall win'.

Yet Hamlet the eloquent knows he is gagged. 'Break, my heart, for I must hold my tongue!' The inventive heightening of speech that comes with convulsive shock, the jumps of 'A very, very—pajock'— 'About my brain!' and 'No, up sword!' spring from an inner conflict that spurs ahead of intent.

> Ere I could make a prologue to my brains,
> They had begun the play.   (5.2.307-8)

Intuition acts almost as a kind of perception; as he reads his own death warrant by the flickering light in the dark and tossing sea cabin, he prepares to copy and improve on a letter of flowery greeting—knowing that a man's life is but no more than to say 'One'; and the elaborately respectful tone of the letter announcing his return gives an enigmatic but menacing echo of this diplomatic flowery speech.

Far beneath the surface of the first two acts, and again at the end, there is some infusion of the ancient stage imagery of the war of angels and devils; but felt only as an ordering of impulse and behaviour, not a doctrine for belief and assent.[14] In Sonnet 194 Shakespeare had used it of his own inner conflict:

> Two loves I have of comfort and despair,
> Which like two spirits do suggest me still:
> The better angel is a man right fair,
> The worser spirit a woman colour'd ill.

This is only one of the conflict systems of Hamlet's elaborate series of plays-within-a-play. It is possible for instance to read it as a human study of mourning; and the absolution of that dreadful solitude that mourning imposes.

The conflicts of human mourning normally follow a fourfold development. In the first phase of shock or disaster, the mourner will not feel anything, but may be deeply numbed and almost paralysed. The second characteristic phase is anger or resentment, sometimes irrationally directed against the dead for having deserted the mourner (the Keening). The third phase is one of restitution, when in phantasy or by some imaginary process of substitution, the mourner tries to replace the dead or re-incorporate them as if they were still alive as part of one's self. The last stage is the acceptance of loss and recovered stability.

In his first soliloquy, Hamlet is still numbed, but grief

for his father passes into rage against his mother, the unworthy remaining half of what to him had been an inseparable double image of authority and love. The third stage of mourning occurs in the voyage to England. Hamlet acts promptly and royally, writing an order in the regal style and sealing it with the Danish signet. And he announces his return by adopting the royal title—'This is I, Hamlet the Dane!' that is, the King of Denmark!

Ophelia's death and burial is that of an English country girl, in some country churchyard; a great lady would have been buried in a vault. She had climbed on the willow tree with her garlands of country flowers, and it is surely in the graveyard by the river that Shakespeare knew so well she is laid when the crowner has sat on her and finds it Christian burial. It is England, as the players' scene is England—quite localized.

And this is where the ghost is finally exorcized. For the graveyard scene is essentially another play within a play. Hamlet picks up the skull of the dead jester. (Burbage was playing opposite Armin, and could they fail to remember Dick Tarlton here?)

Looking into the hollow eyes of the skull as into a crystal, he summons up all the leading characters of the play—the politician that would circumvent God, smooth Claudius flattering his courtiers, Rosencrantz and Guildenstern tossing overseas to an unknown grave, the quibbling lawyer who transmits inheritance, or does not, at the demise of the crown; lastly the figure of a dead martial leader—Alexander the Great—Hamlet the dead King.

The maimed rites begin; Hamlet leaps into the grave, as far from control as ever Claudius had been in the moment of transformation, at this silent meeting with the one he had put from him, and a voice of reproach that sounds like an echo. Again he comes face to face with his wronged 'brother' Laertes. In the very latest version of the play that Shakespeare wrote Hamlet later acknowledges:

> By the image of my cause I see
> The portraiture of his.   (5.2.77-8)

There is little formal stress on the 'images', paintings or mirrors that Fortinbras and Laertes supply for Hamlet. They are not confrontations, like that which the Player gives when Claudius meets his double on the stage, but contrasted modes of action. These figures interact with each other at sword's point. The dynamics of the duel scene bring in the world of time, the mutable variants of Fortune's dispositions. Hamlet, remorsefully contrasting himself with the passions of the tragic stage, or the easy certitudes and hazards of Fortinbras' public action, learns the contingent nature of his own acts, and finally accepts that 'Our indiscretions sometimes serve us well, when our deep plots do pall'. He knows too that 'If it be now, 'tis not to come; if it be not to come, it will be now: if it be not now, yet it will come; the readiness is all'.[15] And so he moves forward to the last play within the play—Claudius' version of *The Mousetrap*, a public entertainment where all the rôles have been cast by the king. By brilliant improvising, Hamlet changes this drama as he goes along. His whole self is directed towards unknown modes of being, focusing the double and dislocated images of his contradictory experience 'impasted by the proper quality of things, by their impermeability, their extension, and that infinity of relations they maintain with other things'.

His dying address from the throne to the whole theatre —for it suddenly widens out in concentric circles to include 'you that are but mutes and audience to this act' the spectators in their galleries—tells them that 'the rest is silence'. But on a stage which had seen the last hour of Dr Faustus, the death scene of Hamlet represents a double triumph: relation between time and eternity is prefigured by the relation between events in life and events in art.

But the contact between actors and audience, their participation, is *not* part of the prefiguration, as it was in the old gild cycles; the action of the moment is hazardous, contingent, self contained, and this is emphasized by artifice.

Drama had come of age, arriving at a new configuration of actors and audience, in their relation to the play and the world beyond. Through a species of dramatic challenges by which the public stages absorbed and eventually modified all other forms of shew, the confluence of private and public traditions of acting had led to the confluence of certain habits and assumptions.[16] In the name of full dramatic illusion, the private identifications which had touched Claudius, which had enlived the moral play by embodying the conflict of passions in identifiable persons (from Skelton's *Magnyfycence* down through the Elizabethan dramas at the Inns of Court and universities) now found itself replaced by the interplay between actors and their *own* function. Fully recognized as a body separate from the audience, guardians of their own craft mystery, they had acquired an identity as actors; the satire is directed not outwards towards the audience but inwards towards themselves and their rivals. The gild that presented and the auditory that attended had learnt their places; the relation of the play to life was that of a fiction, a dream of passion. If the characters portrayed were historical, the spectators might be rapt with 'delight' (the term for complete identification) and 'think [they] see them living'; yet the play is evanescent, at its end the audience are brought back to the theatre in which they sit.

Transformations of this sort may embody the 'second world' of art perhaps with a soul of more lively action than appears in daily existence. (The doctrine had been propounded by Sidney in his praise of poetry's golden world.)

To measure how far drama outstripped life, it is worth turning to the vision of a spiritually disinherited young poet, the Catholic exile and conspirator Anthony Copley, who in 1596 had written of his melancholy, his divided self, in a Spenserian poem entitled defiantly *A Fig for Fortune*.[17]

Here is Hamlet's mood of intransigence, and Hamlet's impulse to revolt; in Copley's world the forms of good and evil are terrifyingly interchangeable, and Copley's attitude towards Queen Elizabeth is schizophrenic. The poem is full of praise for Eliza, 'the Lord's dear dainty'; at the end of the dream poem comes a figure descending in a shower of roses, who resembles Eliza, but is found to be a 'heavenly maid'. Yet earlier the dreamer comes to the Temple of Sion, over whose door is written 'Una, Militans', and is there given St George's Banner, only to find the temple attacked by Doublessa, 'Error's dreary Queen'.

> Like ensigns she opposed to Sion's ensigns,
> Like her pretence of grace and God's high honour,
> Like grapes she did contend grew up her vines,
> And as good gold as Sion's seemed her copper.
> It was but seeming so, not so indeed,
> Her seeming flower was a very weed.

Spenser's Protestant imagery is being inverted; the Catholic Una is attacked by Elizabeth in her anti-papal manifestation. But this is not her only manifestation. The bewilderment with which Hamlet confronts Gertrude's behaviour, which seems to negate her very identity, as well as that of his father, might seem dimly foreshadowed here. Copley is working, however, with a set of static emblems, although his poem describes an interior journey on the 'steed of melancholy' in which visions of monsters and ghosts bedevil him. Half angelical and half serpentine, the Ghost of Cato appears counselling suicide; the Fury Revenge, the 'Phoenix of adversity', counsels for the wrong reasons the glory of martyrdom.

> To act the stately tragic personage . . .
> So should thou close chamelion-like conceal
> Thy tragic shape of horror and revenge.

These emblematic scenes, all familiar and all disorganized, succeed in a vivid and shapeless phantasmagoria. When the white steed replaces the black, it is merely the substitution of one described emblem for another; feeling does not inhere in the object at all.

Hamlet too is filled with contradictions; the Prince speaks of the undiscovered country of death from which no traveller returns, even while the ghost's words are shaping his thoughts of dream beyond life; Claudius says that Hamlet does not sound mad, yet because he is mad he must bewatched. Such contradictions follow the perturbed course of 'thoughts as they rise in the mind'; deep within the play lies the need to tolerate a state of conflict, to reserve an area of mystery.

Hopkins wrote to Robert Bridges:

> By mystery . . . you mean an interesting uncertainty; the uncertainty ceasing, interest ceases also. . . . But a Catholic by mystery means an incomprehensible certainty . . . there are you know some solution to, say, chess problems so beautifully ingenious, some resolutions of suspension so lovely in music that even the feeling of interest is keenest when they are known and over, and for some time survives the discovery. How must it be then when the very answer is the most tantalising statement of the problem and the truth you are to rest in the most pointed putting of the difficulty!
>
> (G. M. Hopkins, *Letters to Bridges*, CX, p. 187)

Harry Levin entitles the three sections of his book on Hamlet 'doubt', 'interrogation' and 'irony'. The doubt is contained, though not resolved; the play itself exemplifies Keats's famous definition, derived from reading Shakespeare, of negative capability—'when a man is capable of being in uncertainties, mysteries, doubts'.

The uncertain universe of *Hamlet* was an enlarged equivalent of the uncertain frame of discourse for the actor. The actor had left behind traditional frameworks— Shakespeare himself had just made one such break. Here he is reinforcing himself with what can be retained, transformed of the older tradition. And it is for this reason, and this spirit, that other and later dramatists have turned to *Hamlet* before any other work for a radical refashioning of their own art, a confrontation of their own dilemma.

iii. The Later 'Hamlets'

Shakespeare's *Hamlet* was an example of traditional work reformed; the play itself may have been subject to that continuous process of reshaping which is so common in the theatre and so hard for the students of the written word to remember. The Bad Quarto reveals some of the things that actors could do to the play and the Folio reveals others. The power of generating and regenerating dramatic experience is suggested by the musings on his own fate that are given to Hamlet only in the latest version, published after Shakespeare's death; but it also contains such emotional intensifications, suggestive of the actors' contributions, as 'O Vengeance!' 'mother, mother' 'pox' and the four-fold 'O, O, O, O', which follows 'the rest is silence' to hold up silence for about ten seconds.

Since this play has acquired the status of myth, impulses to make and remake it often take the form of parody. I shall not discuss the elaborate reformations of the nineteenth century—Byron's for example—which exploit the leading rôle; or the parodies such as *Hamlet Travestie* or *Rosencrantz and Guildenstern* by W. S. Gilbert, but shall conclude with two dramas of the absurd, Alfred Jarry's *Ubu Roi*, and Tom Stoppard's *Rosencrantz and Guildenstern are Dead*.

The greedy and ruthless Ubu, a triumphant idiot figure, at once a father and an infant, was a schoolboy's caricature of his detested schoolmaster. His language is appalling, his habits would make Mr Punch look civilized; Mother Ubu who can match him in insults if not in treachery, urges him on to seize the crown of Poland by murdering the entire Polish royal family. He is therefore among many other things, Claudius; while Bourgrelas, Prince of Poland who escapes the massacre, and eventually with the help of John Sobieski and others regains Poland for the Poles, is of impeccable behaviour like the rest of his slaughtered family. The last scene is on the bridge of a close-hauled schooner on the Baltic:

> PÈRE UBU. . . . at the moment we've passed below the Castle of Elsinore . . . and I'm going to get myself appointed Minister of Finance in Paris.
> MÈRE UBU. O, that's right. Oops, what a bump that was.
> COTICE. That's nothing, we're just doubling the point of Elsinore.

The play was dedicated to Marcel Schwob, the Elizabethan scholar:

Adonc le Père Ubu hocha la poire, donc fut depuis nommé
par les Anglais Shakespeare, et avez de lui sous ce nom maintes
belles tragedies par escargot.

In other words, Ubu is also Shakespeare.
The riot at this drama of the absurd, when it was performed in 1896 has been described by W. B. Yeats who
was at the first night:

> The audience shake their fists at one another and my friend
> whispers to me 'There are often duels after these performances'....
> The chief personage, who is some kind of King, carries for sceptre
> a brush of the kind we use to clean a closet. Feeling bound to
> support the most spirited party, we have shouted for the play....
>
> (*Autobiographies*, pp. 233-4)

This was the first drama of the absurd; the Théâtre
Alfred Jarry, with the Collège de'Pataphysique, founded
in 1949 to study Jarry, have explored the peculiarities of
the antic disposition as the originating theatrical impulse
behind new ritual. Apollinaire, Cocteau, Artaud, Adamov
and Ionesco all derive in a sense from Jarry.[18]
In Stoppard's play the anguish of Hamlet is transferred
to the two little men caught up into his drama. They have
stepped out of their own familiar world into one where a
spun coin comes down heads 92 times. On the way to
Elsinore they meet the players, who are willing to perform
anywhere anytime, with full audience participation. In *The
Rape of the Sabine Women*, the patron may take either rôle,
with encores. Times are bad. But the players themselves
exhibit the greatest vitality, for they have chosen to live the
life of the imagination, and for them there is no anxiety.

GUILDENSTERN. Well, aren't you going to change into your
   costume?
FIRST PLAYER. I never change out of it, sir.
GUILDENSTERN. Always in character.
FIRST PLAYER. That's it.
GUILDENSTERN. Aren't you going to come on?
FIRST PLAYER. I *am* on.   (p. 24)

As in Pirandello's *Six Characters in Search of an Author*, the
play world is the more real one, so here it is the actors who

are more vital than the ordinary men—Samuel Beckett's tramps who have strayed into a tattered, faded production of Shakespeare. When we reach Elsinore, we find that all the original players have shrivelled to ghosts; the first scene is the dumb shew in which Hamlet rushes to Ophelia's closet, but the court is shabby, tawdry, unreal. The anguish of Hamlet is divided between the little men and the players. Rosencrantz and Guildenstern try to play at Questions— 'words, words . . . they're all we have to go on'. They play at being Hamlet; but as soon as they reach their scene with him—'Good lads, how do you both?'—there is a fade out.

'Give us this day our daily mask,' prays Guildenstern, and Rosencrantz repeats his frightened 'I want to go home'.

The scene on the ship bound for England finds them joined by the players. In panic at Hamlet's disappearance, Rosencrantz and Guildenstern open the letter for the second time (they have already read it once) and find the instructions for their own execution. Guildenstern rounds on the first player, stabbing him with his own dagger:

> I'm talking about death. And you've never experienced that. And you cannot act it. You die a thousand casual deaths—with panache, and none of that intensity which squeezes out life . . . and no blood runs cold anywhere. Because as you die, you know you will come back in a different hat. But no one gets up after death—there is no applause—there is only silence and some second-hand clothes. . . .   (p. 92)

After an agonizing death, the player quietly gets up to restrained applause from his fellows. It was a collapsible stage dagger. As at his orders everyone proceeds to die all over the deck:

> Deaths for all ages and occasions; deaths by suspension, convulsion, consumption, incision, execution, asphyxiation, and malnutrition. . . .

the lights dim and go up on the final death scene of Shakespeare's play.

Nevertheless death is precisely what is missing from Stoppard's play. The many different levels of illusion and

142

reality do not include (except in one sentimental passage) the physical level of death. There is nothing to correspond to the graveyard scene. There is acute fear of death as something unknown; but nowhere the smell of earth, the smell of the skull as Hamlet lifts it, the sound of the death rattle, the stench, the worm, the pit. The play does not live on the level of the senses, for it comes out of an alienated world where death is a question mark and takes place in a hospital as a rule. Neither the ghost nor the gravediggers, for very good reasons, appear in the cast. Nevertheless if this play is compared with Stoppard's *Enter a Free Man*, it is obvious that *Hamlet* gives a more powerful boost to the imagination than *The Wild Duck*, with its attic and its inventor.

The craftsmanship of *Hamlet* not only allows but demands the fullest collaboration of actors and spectators. A whole life is condensed to the two hours' traffic of the stage, and though there is a void at the centre of Hamlet the man, and a ghost at the centre of *Hamlet* the play, this is where, in the words of another poet, 'words, after speech, reach into the silence'.

CHAPTER VIII

BLACKFRIARS:
THE PAGEANT OF TIMON OF ATHENS

W HEN an Elizabethan craftsman printed off a
volume, painted an inn-sign or erected a
gorgeous playing place in the fields, each took
traditional forms. Adapting to local need, adding fine
touches, he followed what as an apprentice he had learned,
so that we recognize at once the proportions of an arch that
Ben Jonson might have pointed, the shape of embroidered
gauntlets that John Shakespeare of Stratford might have
cut and sewn. John's eldest son too was a craftsman; his
models, though not defined by classical rules, might be
recognized and judged in the playing by his audience, as
well as by the actors' gild or fellowship of which, by the
early seventeenth century, he was a master. His play of
Timon opens with two craftsmen, Painter and Poet, con-
ducting an informed discussion on their work; 'Here is a
touch; is't good?' asks one.

Timon of Athens, a work of profound and disturbed feeling, of broken and uneven magnificence, is perhaps not a
full play at all (and maybe that was why Shakespeare's
friends did not originally intend to insert it in his collected
works, but slipped it in to fill a gap). There is no direct
evidence of when it was written or whether it was ever
staged. It is the only play in the 'Tragic' section of the
Folio not entitled 'The Tragedie of . . .' nor yet like the
tragical histories, 'The Life and Death of . . .' but simply
'The Life of Timon of Athens'. Let us call it 'no play but
a shew'[1]; an experimental scenario for an indoor dramatic
pageant. In modern terms it might be called an anti-shew;
in Jacobean ones: *A Dramatick Shew of the Life of Timon
of Athens, wherein his progress through the Four Seasons, as
also through the Four Humours in an earthly Zodiack is set forth,
together with the City Vice of Usury in diverse Senators, the*

144

snarling asperity of prideful Scholars, and the mercenary decline
of Poetry and Painting in this latter age. All displayed in sundry
variety of dramatick utterance, chiefly by way of Paradoxes.

Like another masque of the four seasons, now lost, it was
'for speeches as good as a play'[2]; but in plotting entirely
different, being emblematic rather than dramatic. The
piece describes an arc—a double rainbow or solar year; the
rising half is divided into scenes which are set in opposition
with the falling half. Progress through this arc is partly a
progress through certain dramatic forms, from the old
Interlude to the contemporary Masque, some of which is
very clever parody, like the Hollis Street sequence in
Ulysses. But in the second half a more poetic and lyric
rhythm of times and seasons emerges, with the absolute
dominance of the hero, by whose passing the life of Nature
and Man is united. Two patterns, the theatrical and the
cosmic, can be discerned throughout, although the first
predominated initially, the second finally.

Echoes of particular lines sound across the divide;
Apemantus' blasphemous sneer 'He wrought better that
made the Painter; and yet he's but a filthy piece of work'
is repeated by Timon; and there are others. The soldier
condemned for violent avenging of a wrong is matched
by 'poor straggling soldiers' turned outlaws.[3] Timon, in
his great speech abjuring the world, the hinge upon which
the whole play turns, for twenty lines invokes moral disorder and chaos on Athens, for the next twenty physical
pestilence. The Walls of Athens are conjured to sink in
the earth (perhaps they did); then confusion invoked on
Athenians 'both within and out that wall'. It is symmetrical
as a tirade in Corneille.

Yet we miss the full Shakespearean rhythmic tide, the
play of voice against voice, the rippling movement glinting
with imagery half explicit and half submerged, the inter-
lacing. Instead opposition sharpens to paradox; 'Thou sun
that comfort'st, burn!' 'Destruction, fang mankind!'
'Graves only be men's works and death their gain.' Latterly
this curt style alternates with Timon's passionate invoca-
tions to the primary powers of sun, earth, gold, sea, the

gods in their natural incarnations; with appeals to invisible powers. From the first, he is a man of unfocused impulse; nothing is said of his family, his age or the manner of his death. Other characters relate to him, not to each other. Unlike earlier or later Prodigals, Timon courts no mistress; the World and not the Flesh is his undoing. In the first half, women appear only as silent dancers—Amazons (that is, warriors and strangers), though led by blind Cupid. Choric figures make a brief appearance and vanish; in this drama of the gaps, however, there *was* a collaborator. Not the literary hack once so popular with disintegrators, but the one collaborator with whom the poet worked in all his major plays, I mean the Painter who probably designed the production, and inevitably acted the lead—Richard Burbage.

This very brief work's deceptive simplicity has tempted —even seemed to justify—interpretations as confident as they are diverse. Some hold it a black comedy, with Northrop Frye—'*The Merchant of Venice* seen through Shylock's eyes'.[4] But such elementary ignorance of money and of the place of competitive spirit in public life as the hero betrays have provoked others to ask more bluntly 'Why is he such a fool?' Wilson Knight, who had acted in it, asserts that *Timon* transcends and includes *Hamlet, Lear, Othello* and *Troilus and Cressida*.

Dover Wilson terms it 'the still-born twin of *Lear*'; Chambers, Greg, the last two editors, Maxwell and Oliver (and nearly everyone else) think it unfinished; Clifford Leech and John Wain see it as 'not the last and least of the tragedies but the doubtful harbinger of the Romances'.[5] I think, as the children say, they are getting warmer.

Part of the opening scene serves as Induction or Prologue, recalling the spectacular old court interlude of *Liberality and Prodigality*, where Prodigality scaled the height of Fortune's Hill, only to be thrust down with a halter round his neck.

Timon's court poet is writing a 'rough work' of this sort, depicting one of 'Lord Timon's frame'. The Painter says

unkindly that the theme is too common; and indeed though
the old interlude had been revived at Court in Elizabeth's
last years, the whole conception *was* about fifty years
behind the times in Jacobean London. Sage judgements at
this level could have been found in a Prodigal play written
when Shakespeare was an infant.

> A common saying, better envy than ruth,
> I had rather they should spite than pity me;
> For the old saying nowadays proveth truth,
> Nought have, nought set by, as daily we see . . .
> As by mine own father an example I may take,
> He was beloved of all men and kept a good house
> While riches lasted, but when that did forsake,
> There was no man that did set by him a louse . . . . [6]

Timon's faithful steward gives this same old saying a
mordant twist as he glosses the Sermon on the Mount,
'Love your enemies':

> Grant I may ever love—and rather woo
> Those that would mischief me than those that do.
>
> (4.3.470-1)

New twists to old saws, sardonically emphasized by rhyme,
are found everywhere. That *Timon* is a warning mirror,
reflecting the plight of spendthrift nobility, was suggested
nearly twenty years ago, before the writings of Trevor
Roper and Lawrence Stone developed so fully the econo-
mic crisis of the Elizabethan aristocracy. This is a plausible
and tempting reading for the first half. The highly ceremonious entry of Timon, to the sound of trumpets,
'addressing himself courteously to every suitor', introduces
a series of acts traditionally recognized as Liberal rather
than Prodigal; he redeems a debtor from prison and gives
a dowry to a servant—singled out as favourite forms of
philanthropy by the historian of London charities, W. K.
Jordan.[7]

Hospitality rules the feast—and another Interlude had
shewn the good old man Hospitality murdered by Usury.[8]
Timon's courtesy and generosity, his noble tastes for hunt-

ing and the arts draw from his poet a parody of one of
Shakespeare's greater sonnets:

> When we for recompence have prais'd the vile,
> It stains the glory in that happy verse
> Which aptly sings the good.   (1.1.15-17)

Yet before this, almost the opening words suggest a darker
picture: a Jeweller and a Merchant (or Mercer) accompany
the Poet and Painter as all converge upon their magnificent
Patron.

> See,
> Magic of bounty, all these spirits thy power
> Hath conjur'd to attend.   (1.1.5-7)

Good spirits were not conjur'd into a circle; later the Fool
defines this universal spirit as Lust; and Plutus, the chthonic god, is named as Timon's steward.[9]

The old interludes had implied a society bound by personal ties of servant and lord, the hierarchial traditions of
great households—except at court, now largely obsolescent
and ceremonious (though players found livery service a
protection against the law). But (Paradox Number Two)
there is a fracture between the nature of society implied
and the setting presented—which is republican Athens.
Timon's friends owe him no pledged service, and he incurs
no obligations of lordship, except where he retains loyalty,
in his household. All are Citizens ... financiers ... Greeks;
or rather, as Terence Spencer observed, they are Merrygreeks.[10]

Elizabethan Englishmen were not keen on the Greeks.
To descendants of Pious Aeneas, inhabitants of Troyno-
vant, they might almost have appeared as hereditary
enemies. Greeks were thought of as convivial and dissipated
because the Romans saw them that way; a 'Grecian' or
'Merrygreek' was Elizabethan slang for a roysterer. Greeks
also being twisters, liars and cheats, Timon's friends were
merely living up to the national character. The presence
of Alcibiades alone would make the point—Alcibiades,
who, as Plutarch says, could transform himself into all
shapes, more easily than the chameleon.[11] Shakespeare's

main source, Lucian's *Dialogue of Timon*, in its sardonic deflation of gods and men, is echoed in the rancour of Apemantus, who is used by Timon and his friends as a kind of whetstone of wit. Dialogue with this cynic philosopher consists only of questions, which the Senators, Timon, even the servants, throw him teasingly to make him snarl, as dogs might be tarred on to worry at a bear-baiting. The constant play on the epithet 'dog' almosts suggests some memory of the savage bull and bear rings; though of course question and answer was still the recognized mode of academic instruction, and merry invective a well tried device of the academic arena. 'Who comes here; will you be chid?' asks Timon, to be snapped at with a twist to the old proverb, 'Sheep eat men';[12]

TIMON. Wilt dine with me, Apemantus?
APEMANTUS. No; I eat not lords.   (1.1.204-5)

This first hint that Timon is being devoured by his friends echoes through the Banquet of Sense which follows, and the Masque to feast the eyes. It is a triumph of the element of Air; music of the lutes contrasted with the more gloomy hautboys; airy dances, airy promises—celestial but childish like blind Cupid, the presiding God.[13]

In Act 2, Riot and Waste sound the autumnal themes of decline; in an antic scene where Cupid is replaced by the Fool, servant of a city whore, puzzles about identity are raised. Folly, a traditional attendant on the Prodigal Son and Lady Pecunia or Fortune the Whore, here waits at Timon's door, with the philosopher and some usurers' men, 'bawds between want and gold'. A riddling game of question and answer starts, and develops into a verbal dance of catch-as-catch-can.

VARRO'S SERVANT. How dost, fool?
APEMANTUS. Dost dialogue with thy shadow?   (2.2.55-6)

To underline the rhetorical formality the servants speak in chorus, asking 'Who are we, Apemantus?' 'Where's the fool now?' asks Cephis, to be smartly answered 'He last asked the question.' In the second half of the play, a similar riddling game is played between Timon, the Painter and Poet, when both are proved villains; in each case the players move about in ballet order.[14]

Gradually Timon is transformed from Liberality of the old interlude to the Dupe of the new city comedy of Marston or Middleton, the Jonathan Millers of the time. As he paid the debtor's fine, Timon claimed:

> I am not of that feather to shake off
> My friend when he must need me. (1.1.103-4)

but as the first creditor soon remarks:

> When every feather sticks in his own wing
> Lord Timon will be left a naked gull
> Which flashes now a Phoenix. (2.1.30-2)

A naked fledgling (the current meaning of *gull*) is suddenly exposed by the Fool when the usurers' men ask in chorus 'How does your mistress?' 'She's e'en setting on water to scald such chickens as you are' (2.2.73-4). The obscenities could be considerably extended in action.

A farcial *Comedy of Timon* the Merrygreek survives in a fragile manuscript,[15] which must have come from legal circles, probably from the Inner Temple. Timon is shewn in love, and he is given as rival a foolish City Heir, Gelasimus of the Golden Hill;[16] there is also a parody of Timon's last banquet. This little skit (if one assumes that even nonsense need not be pointless) shews how powerful was the effect of Shakespeare's bitter comedy; but it makes fun of dons, and the dons have retaliated by treating it with the utmost seriousness, solemnly arguing for Shakespeare's indebtedness or postulating a common source.

The mood in Act 3 of Shakespeare's play, where Timon is kept off stage, is that of Apemantus; in a brilliant series of sketches, the creditors are shewn one at a time; Timon's ideal of 'a band of brothers commanding one another's fortunes' is shewn to be but 'a dream of friendship' and he is dunned by the beneficiaries of his hospitality till even their servants condemn it as ingratitude 'worse than stealth'. Ceremony cloaks hard legal bargains; a man with Timon's meat in him refuses the courtesy of a welcoming drink to his messenger. One touch of nature makes the whole world kin, as Shakespeare had previously remarked; the band of brothers act with remarkable unanimity. They are ironically realized in most sophisticated writing as natural comedians in a sick jest, each with his own line. Lucullus turns back the messenger for a loan with bluff worldliness:

> La, la, la, la. 'Nothing doubting' says he? Alas, good lord; a noble gentleman 'tis, if he would not keep so good a house. Many a time and oft I ha' dined with him, and told him on't, and come again to supper to him o' purpose to have him spend less; and yet he would embrace no counsel, take no warning by my coming. Every man has his fault, and honesty is his. . . . I have observed thee always for a towardly prompt spirit, give thee thy due, and one that knows what belongs to reason, and canst use the time well, if the time use thee well. . . . Here's three solidares for thee. Good boy, wink at me and say thou saw'st me not.
>
> (3.1.22-45)

The 'straight man', flinging back the money, is written off; 'Ha, now I see thou art a Fool, and fit for thy master' (3.1.49-50). A second usurer smoothly blames Lucullus, and when trapped by a like request is dexterous enough to invent his own bland lie.

> What a wicked beast was I, to disfurnish myself, against such a good time, when I might ha' shewed myself honourable. . . . Servilius, now before the gods, I am not able to do—the more beast, I say—I was sending to use Lord Timon myself, these gentlemen can witness; but I would not for the wealth of Athens I had done it now. Commend me bountifully to his good lordship, and I hope his honour will conceive the fairest of me because I have no power to be kind. . . . I'll look you out a good turn, Servilius.
>
> (3.2.45-61)

The last usurer strikes a loftier note, taking umbrage because he was not first asked; his verse jingles like false money:

> With their faint reply, this answer join:
> Who bates my honour shall not know my coin.
>
> (3.3.27-8)

Cannibalistic imagery emerges as Timon rages, crying 'Cut my heart in sums', 'Tell out my blood for drachmas'; but his Shylocks have the law of their side, a soldier (type of unrewarded desert in the old interludes) being sentenced to death in full Senate for avenging his wrongs in blood; Alcibiades banished for pleading his cause.[17] Rigorous penalty for a choleric act shews Timon's danger if his creditors should prove his judges.

However, he can act a part as well as they; to his last feast, a shew within a shew, he summons his betrayers, and as they explain, 'conjures' them till again in a predatory ring, from divers doors they 'needs must appear' (3.6.11-12). The Last Feast is a stage banquet, 'only painted like his varnished friends' (4.2.35-6) which marks the moment of transformation, of cataclysmic change, when passion mutates Timon into a new creature. In his Grace to the Gods, 'You great Benefactors', he attempts a godlike indifference of condemnation, lapsing into rage as he contemplates the bestial encroaching upon the human.

> For these my present friends, as they are to me nothing, so in nothing bless them, and to nothing are they welcome. Uncover, dogs, and lap. (3.6.81-4)

Timon sets the pack in flight from his stage feast of stones and smoking water, by falling on them like an angry Jove. In imitation of the habit of showering guests at feasts with gilded sweetmeats or the like (this happens in *Liberality and Prodigality* at one point)[18] Timon hurls stones of vengeance, darts the forky fire of his paradoxes, arraigns Fortune in her servants' folly.

> Courteous destroyers, affable wolves, meek bears,
> You fools of fortune, trencher friends, time's flies,
> Cap and knee slaves, vapours and minute jacks.
> (3.6.94-6)

The farcial *Comedy of Timon*, which burlesques this scene, four or five times calls Timon an earthly Jove or Jupiter, and he opens the banquet scene saying he is equal to Jove, flings the stones with the words:

If I Jove's horrid thunderbolt did hold,
Within my hand, thus, thus would I dart it. (p. 75)

The stones *he* hurls are shaped like *artichokes*! In contemporary iconography Jove's bolt, to the irreverent, resembles nothing so much as an elongated artichoke; indeed
some may be found in A. B. Cook's *Zeus*, with a 'Rain of
Stones' and 'Rain of Food' (III, 482-506).

Blind Cupid, Folly, Jove; Desire, Vanity, Judgment;
these are the presiding deities of the first acts. This last
ritual scene evokes stage hell also; 'Burn house, sink
Athens!' as the deviser of Cupid's masque plays his last
pageant. Later, Prospero was to use the same device of an
anti-feast to convict the three 'men of sin' through the
avenging Harpy, Ariel. The assembly bundles off, but the
last scene of this macabre tragicomedy shews them re-
trieving their booty, and defining Timon's condition by
that simple label which deprives him at once of civil rights
and human status—madness.

> 1 LORD. He's a mad lord, and nought but humour sways him.
> He gave me a jewel t'other day and now he has beat it out of
> my hat. Did you see my jewel?
> 3 LORD. Did you see my cap? . . .
> 2 LORD. Lord Timon's mad.
> 3 LORD. I feel't upon my bones.
> 4 LORD. One day he gives us diamonds, next day stones.
> (3.6.110-20)

Governed by his heart rather than his reason, his sense
of community expressed in the simple forms of feasting
and hunting, Timon has been ruled by humour; first dominated by the youthful, spring-time, airy, sanguine temper,
then by hot choler. Only his servants 'feel their master's
passion' as they embrace and part 'into a sea of air', into
oblivion; the Steward indicts Fortune and defends Timon's
fine impulses (his 'blood') and the quality of his imagination
(his 'mind')—

> Strange, unusual blood,
> When man's worst sin is, he does too much good . . .
> My dearest lord, blessed to be most accurst,

Rich only to be wretched, thy great Fortunes
Are made thy great afflictions.   (4.2.38-42)

Timon as noble Liberality, and as Hospitality, reflects
the moral interludes; Timon, the Gull, the Merrygreek,
reflects that new bitter comedy where morality was
mocked.[19] Critics like Collins and Pettit see only the
one, critics like Campbell and Frye only the other; both
exist, successively, because Timon is a rôle and not a
character.

At this point I should like to define the nature of a shew,
in respect of those elements found in *Timon* (my definition
is largely based on Ben Jonson): *A shew, developing as
distinct numbers or pageants, laid flatly against each other, its
scenes and characters are united by rhythmic contrast. Costume is
gorgeous and symbolic; speech in the form of set orations or brisk
debate; one leading character may dominate (and there are likely
to be few if any women characters). Contrast and display are
the vehicles, times and seasons, vices and virtues, gods and
goddesses the subjects; the script is short, designed for one production only.*[20]

In part II, the proverbial Timon *Misanthropos*, socially
a freak and a monster, a kind of fairground Caliban in
popular view, turns away from the walled City and prays:

Grant as Timon grows, his hate may grow
To the whole race of mankind, high and low.
                    (4.1.39-40)

He grows. Now, as in the second part of a Japanese
Noh play, a figure who had appeared merely human
assumes a godlike stature, the scene around him shines
transparent. We pass from the City to the Cave (for in the
play, place is symbolic and of supreme importance). For
ceremony, a hermitage; in place of Fortune the City whore,
the common whore of mankind—glittering yellow gold
that at once and miraculously, Timon uncovers. With the
discovery of this dazzling hoard that can make black white,
wrong right, corrupt all men and for which he upbraids the
gods, Timon's new identity is suggested. Once before in
the glitter of Cupid's masque, Apemantus had exclaimed

'Men shut their doors against a setting sun' (1.2.145) and
as Timon hid from his creditors a servant observed:

> The days are waxed shorter with him.
> You must consider that a prodigal's course
> Is like the sun's but not like his recoverable.
> I fear
> 'Tis deepest winter in Lord Timon's purse.
>
> (3.4.11-15)

Solar man in his auspicious rising and in his eclipsing
cave bears a natural affinity with the metal Sol, or Gold; he
may play the part of the supreme Sky God, wielding his
thunderbolts against offenders. His compulsive bounty is
godlike, his gifts breed other gifts; but this is not 'an
autumn that grows the more by reaping'. The devouring
greed of his fair-weather friends[21] belongs to a nether
Zodiack; they also 'do their nature'. Interrelation of plane-
tary, alchemical, mythological and psychological influence
in the renaissance doctrine of man was clarified recently by
the great work of Klibansky, Saxl, and Panovsky, *Saturn
and Melancholy*, which described the third phase of earth,
melancholy, winter into which Timon is now entering.
But justification for associating him with Jove and the metal
Sol in a very special way is found in the most obvious place
—Lucian's *Dialogue of Timon*,[22] Shakespeare's source;
where Zeus sends Plutus to the exiled Timon, and an
enthusiastic flatterer proposes that Timon's statue shall be
set up beside Athena's with a thunderbolt in his hand and
an aureole of rays. (The farcial *Comedy of Timon* takes over
this.) Now come Shakespeare's great appeals to the sky-
father, earth-mother, and to all-corrupting gold, child of
the sun's loins and the earth's womb, in tragic phrases
that eventually caught the ear of young Karl Marx.[23]

> O blessed breeding sun, draw from the earth
> Rotten humidity; below thy sister's orb
> Infect the air. . . .   (4.3.1-3)

> Common mother, thou
> Whose womb unmeasurable and infinite breast

Teems and feeds all . . .
Teem with new monsters. . . .

(4.3.178-80, 191)

Gold, yellow, glittering, precious gold?
This yellow slave
Will knit and break religions; bless th'accurst;
Make the hoar leprosy ador'd; place thieves. . . .
Come, damned earth,
Thou common whore of mankind, . . . I will make thee
Do thy right nature   (4.3.26-45)

O thou sweet king-killer and dear divorce
Twixt natural son and sire, thou bright defiler
Of Hymen's purest bed, thou valiant Mars,
Thou ever young, fresh, lov'd and delicate wooer. . . .
Think thy slave man rebels, and by thy virtue
Set them into confounding odds, that beasts
May have the world in empire.   (4.3.383-94)

This rôle touches the very frontiers of the articulate, the
borders of what can be known of the state of dereliction,
where conflicts are revealed so deep and elemental, so
painful and relatively inaccessible, that only through the
most lightly established form can they be projected in
words. As tragic exile, Timon retreats deep in a wintry
world, a cinder world; it is winter not only in his purse but
in his heart, and this chthonic world is his alone.

> Descend lower, descend only
> Into a world of perpetual solitude,
> World not world, but that which is not world,
> Internal darkness, deprivation
> And destitution of all property,
> Desiccation of the world of sense,
> Evacuation of the world of fancy,
> Inoperancy of the world of spirit.
>   (T. S. Eliot, 'Burnt Norton', *Four Quartets*).

The pathology of misanthropy balances the worldliness
of Athens; its *mode* is quite different. As tragic pageant it
reverses the tableaux while completing the cycle of seasons
and humours[24]—through winter to revival, through melancholy to the phlegmatic immobility of the tomb.

Visitants come to try Timon. First the messenger of
Jove's pestilence, the traitor Alcibiades with his two
whores. To the 'High-viced City' of Pestilence Timon
speeds them in a passion of hatred; for although he later
declared that should Athens be sacked 'I cannot choose
but tell him that I care not'—yet he does care. In an essay on
the weeping and the laughing philosophers, Democritus
and Heraclitus, Montaigne observed 'look what a man
hateth, the same thing he takes to heart; Timon wished all
evil might light on us; he was passionate in desiring our
ruin'.[25]
The indifferent philosopher is represented here by
Apemantus, of all men most hateful now to Timon.[26]
Apemantus, whose name means 'feeling no pain', is tied to
the City he despises—seeing the wild woods only as some-
where that is not Athens, Timon as no more than the Prodigal among husks. He bids Timon return to the City; he is

> . . . a madman so long, now a fool. What, think'st
> That the bleak air, thy boisterous Chamberlain,
> Will put thy shirt on warm? (4.3.222-4)

He does not understand the irreversible nature of the
mutation; that Timon is not enforced by lack of gold. When
Timon proclaims that he would hand over the empire of the
world to beasts, whose mutual predatory hatred he describes as a vicious Hobbesian hierarchy of fear, Apemantus
prudently qualifies his assent:

> Would 'twere so,
> But not till I am dead. (4.3.394-5)

With the philosopher, Timon bandies insults; with the
'poor straggling soldiers' whom the world's ingratitude has
outlawed he proves pedantically and obsessively that even
inorganic nature is corrupt as man and cruel as beasts. As
in Part I the flesh he had nourished turned against him,
so now the sun, moon, sea, earth live by mutual theft. This
is a vision of total depravity. Momentarily he recovers at
the sight of his faithful Steward in tears—'surely thou
wast born of woman?'—but a new revulsion is phrased in

a strange pageant image. When James entered London to his coronation, he was greeted with a pageant of the Five Senses, under which Detraction and Oblivion lay asleep; but now

Pity's sleeping.[27]   (4.3.488)

Yet the countermovement has already begun, a reconciliation through death, if not with man, yet with the elemental powers:

> Then, Timon presently prepare thy grave,
> Lie where the light foam of the sea may beat
> Thy gravestone daily; make thine epitaph
> That death in me at others' lives may laugh.
>
> (4.3.379-81)

This is the moment when Death, Winter and Spring meet together, when 'critic Timon laughs at idle toys' (*Love's Labour's Lost*, 4.3.166).

It was the belief of the Pythagoreans, as Bacon noted:

> that the soul of the world was one entire, perfect and living creature; insomuch as Apollonius of Tyarna, a Pythagorean prophet, affirmed that the ebbing and flowing of the sea was the respiration of the world, drawing in water as breath and putting it forth again. They went on and inferred that if the world were a living creature it had a soul and a spirit, which they also held, calling it *spiritus mundi.* (*Sylva Sylvarum*, Century X, 900)

Early in the last act, the Steward learns in the last and greatest of Timon's paradoxes—in Words for the Lenten season[28]—that his master has passed the nadir of his winter world.

> Why, I was writing of mine epitaph.
> It will be seen tomorrow. My long sickness
> Of health and living now begins to mend,
> And nothing brings me all things. (5.1.185-8)

As he sinks into his ocean grave, Solar Man, now absolute for death, regains unity with 'the moving waters at their priestlike task of pure ablution round earth's human shores'. The last of the four elements, proper to the latest season of the Zodiack, to the signs of Aquarius and Pisces,

158

to the phlegmatic condition of death, receives Timon, and 'vast Neptune' mourns him[29] (5.4.38). I cannot think that in any ordinary play the hero's death scene would be omitted; no Elizabethan audience nor any Elizabethan actor would tolerate such a thing. But here, as a tomb by the turbulent sea verge is set up as 'Athens' oracle', other speech than this mute witness is abjured:

> Lips, let four words go by, and language end:
> What is amiss, plague and infection mend;
> Graves only be men's works, and death their gain;
> Sun, hide thy beams; Timon hath done his reign.
>
> (5.1.219-22)

How else could this escape the paranoia of Housman's suicide with his eighteenpenny knife: 'I need but stick it in my heart ... and all you folk will die'? If Timon is not to recall the death of Bully Bottom and another wood near Athens and 'Tongue, lose thy light, Moon, take thy flight' there must be a level on which his death is a cosmic abdication; and another on which Alcibiades can shed human tears on 'faults forgiven'. Lear outstretched on the rack of the tough world is recalled when the poor soldier reads the inscription on the cave; Timon had 'outstretched his span'. His death was then natural and not a suicide; in plague time a man was indeed known to dig his own grave and lie down in it to die.[30]

The oracular tomb bears an epitaph in secret characters which the not illiterate messenger cannot decipher but takes to Alcibiades for interpretation. It witholds, then yields the very name of Timon—two epitaphs conflated, Shakespeare had not made a choice, observe the critics intelligently. Rejection of humanity, prohibition of a pause to mourn forbids use of the most conspicuous extravagance and self-advertisement of Jacobean nobility; Shakespeare's own handsome tomb bears a rude and popular bit of cursing which has effectually kept vandals from digging him up— the sort of thing a gravedigger could read. Timon's ever-lasting mansion was, even so, far from man. The savage and Lucianic mood is found in the last two encounters of

Timon with Athenians—the Poet and Painter, then the Senators.

As if to a shrine, Poet and Painter advance deviously through the perspective of the woods, deciding 'in all honesty' to promise some offerings that will unlock Timon's new hoard. The Painter observes 'To promise is most courtly and fashionable; Performance is a kind of will or testament that argues a great sickness in his judgement that makes it' and the Poet thinks up a moral satire depicting Timon himself, condemning flattery. Overhearing them, Timon sardonically acknowledges the source of attraction:

> What a god's gold,
> That he is worshipped in a baser temple
> Than where swine feed.   (5.1.46-8)

If mordant self-satire be the note earlier, what is here? Burbage and Shakespeare once collaborated to design an impresa for a noble lord. If *Timon* were designed for the new Blackfriars Theatre Burbage might have painted in the heavens such a Zodiack as Heywood describes in his *Apology for Actors*. Timon mentions the 'marbled mansion all above' (4.3.191), and such gaudy images would give the Painter's reinforcement to the imagery of this poem. Emblems of the five senses, the four seasons, the four humours and the twelve signs of the Zodiack were commonplace in court masques between 1604 and 1609 and even the *Comedy of Timon* has the Seven Stars—as an innsign (*ed. cit.* p. 36). Now Timon stones both craftsmen off, challenging them to transmute his missiles: 'You are an alchemist, make gold of that' (5.1.113) he cries to the Poet. What is Shakespeare doing here to himself?

As the Senators come to restore Timon's fortune, and beg his return, he kneels in prayer

> Thou sun that comfort'st, burn!   (5.1.130)

Here follows the incident that Plutarch first told of Timon; to help them escape massacre by the knives of Alcibiades' cut-throats, Timon offers a tree growing near his cave,

on which in the sequence of degrees, Athenians may come
and ceremoniously hang themselves. The pageant scene
here presented has gone unrecognized though it is famous
—the last and deadliest temptation with which Spenser
confronts the Knight of Holiness—'a man of Hell, that
calls himself Despair'. Despair, in Spenser,

> his dwelling has, low in a hollow cave
> Far underneath a craggy cliff ypight
> Dark, doleful, dreary, like a greedy grave. . . .
> And all about old stocks and stubs of trees
> Whereon nor fruit nor leaf was ever seen,
> Did hang upon the rocky, ragged knees,
> On which had many wretches hanged been.
>
> (*F.Q.* I. IX. xxxiii-iv)

Traditionally at climax of old plays, especially Prodigal
plays, the figure of Despair appeared with rope and knife—
from Skelton's *Magnyfycence* to the Usurer in Greene's
Looking Glass for London.[31] Spenser may indeed be recalling
the pageants that lie behind *Timon*, who offers Despair's
bounty:

> Tell them, that to ease them of their griefs, . . .
> Their pangs of love, with other incident throes
> That nature's fragile vessel doth sustain
> In life's uncertain voyage, I will some kindness do them.
>
> (5.1.196-201)

They had been commended to the 'prosperous gods' as
thieves to keepers—to greedy gods, battening on misery's
propitiating fees; Timon's godlike everlasting mansion lies
beneath the evershifting tides, not in the heavens.

Life begins on the other side of despair—the maxim of
Sartre would not have seemed unfamiliar to the seventeenth
century, for something like it was found in the writings of
Luther.[32] To the end, then, the figure of Timon remains
ambiguous and paradoxical.

To appreciate the general form I should like to give an
account of one indoor pageant which Shakespeare might
have recollected. Dekker's and Ford's *The Sun's Darling*
survives only in a later version, but shews how Raybright,

Child of the Sun, riots through the four seasons in company with Humour and Folly, only to meet in the depth of winter with the royal maiden Bounty.

Paradoxical union of death and festivity is better displayed in Nashe's *Summer's Last Will and Testament*, given in the autumn of the great plague year 1592 at the Croydon manor of the Archbishop of Canterbury. This pageant, often thought so formless that I may be suspected of justifying lack of form in Shakespeare by lack of form in Nashe adapted the old country Harvest Play in a mixture of naïvety and sophistication.

It is divided into two halves—Summer's Farewell and Winter's Invective—symbolized by the two famous songs, 'Spring, the sweet spring, is the year's pleasant King' and 'Adieu, farewell earth's bliss', a plague prayer (*Timon* is full of plague imagery and there was a bad outbreak in 1607).

> Brightness falls from the air,
> Queens have died young and fair,
> Dust hath closed Helen's eye.
> I am sick, I must die:
> Lord, have mercy on us.

At first, dying Summer's officers are called to their reckonings—spendthrift Spring, proud Sol, churlish Harvest, Bacchus the Merrygreek, Orion the Hunter. Only the hermit of the Equinox is praised. Winter denounces Autumn, Summer's heir:

> A weatherbeaten bankrupt ass it is,
> That scatters and consumeth all he hath,
> Each one do pluck from him without control. . . .
>
> (ll. 1,247-9)

Winter is a usurer, his elder son Christmas a Puritan and a 'snudge', his younger son ('the veriest dog in Christendom' who hates 'the air, the fire, the spring, the year') is thrust down into hell. Winter rails on philosophers, scholars, poets, all who 'thought the Sun and Moon and stars were gods' and who in a 'voluntary wretched poverty' expressed it by 'contempt of gold, thin fare and lying hard'.

A Fool presides over the whole play, and his incursion into the action divides the two halves of this hotchpotch of verse and prose. The 'rough' verse and prose of Shakespeare's piece would be more than justified by comparison with Nashe: it is part of the same tradition.

This shew exhibits in common with *Timon* a seasonal theme, processional movement, a mixture of monologue and scholastic debate or invective; division in contrasted halves; structure by means of apposition, rather than development of a plot. But of course the Jacobean Shakespeare would be actually competing against Jonson's court masques, the *Masque of Beauty*, or *of Queens*; these gorgeous shews, composed for James I's queen, in their brilliance reached almost Florentine splendour.[33] The first of them, given at Hampton Court, offered a Cave of Sleep and a Temple of Pallas, where the Queen appeared in Amazonian sort, as one courtier wrote, with tucked-up skirts 'not so much below the knee but that we might see a woman had both feet and legs, which I never knew before'.

Towards the end of 1609, Shakespeare's company opened an indoor theatre at the Great Parliament Chamber in Blackfriars—the first time any men's company had enjoyed such a privilege. This move from the medieval open air stage to the ancestor of all modern stages is one of the most important events in English dramatic history. The magnificent building, quite the equal of Hampton Court or the hall of Trinity College, had known a tragic pageant of real life which Shakespeare later staged—the divorce of Katharine of Aragon was enacted here. Irwin Smith, in a recent study, notes that after they opened Blackfriars, more masques were staged by the King's Men; Shakespeare returned to a habit unused since his early court comedies; and Smith thinks *Timon* a Globe play 'written with Blackfriars in mind'.[34] J. M. Nosworthy goes further, and terms it a conscious attempt to write spectacular tragedy, either for Blackfriars or the Court.[35] I think it essentially an indoor play as both décor, movement and nature of the chief rôle imply.

Contrast between the City and Woods is central, place

is specially significant, and Timon as Wild Man of the Woods takes a pageant rôle of great antiquity. The cave with its trees was also a well-known pageant device; revolves or *periaktoi* could have been used for this, for the practicable walls on which two senators appear, and for the great spectacular novelty and climax of the tomb. Twice the spectators had been informed the tomb was by the sea, and Alcibiades confirms it; there *must* therefore have been a sea provided, either by waterworks or a wave machine, such as the one Jonson used at court (an example survives in the Theatre Royal at Drottningholm). On the other hand, the Athenian scenes feel inclosed; characters move formally, advancing from several doors into a circle, embracing to part several ways. The banquets involve only token numbers; there are no battle scenes, no mobs. Ceremonious welcome and leavetaking is accompanied by trumpets; the actual music for the masque (music was a tradition at Blackfriars) survives in manuscript at the British Museum,[36] and adds to the probability that the play was completed. Described as 'The Amazonians' Masque', it is written in a hand that Dr Brett, of King's College, would date as between 1610 and 1620. Music for *Macbeth* and *The Tempest* is also there. The lutes are elegant (but there would have been acoustic trouble at the Globe), the hautboys sinister.

In part II, the lonely Man with a Spade is a powerful symbolic figure, whom Shakespeare had used in the gardeners' scene in *King Richard II* and the gravediggers' scene in *Hamlet*; 'old Adam's likeness', he typifies at once toil and mortality; he is lowly as Jove is lofty.

A long perspective of woodland is suggested by Alcibiades' fife and drum approach, the delayed departure of Apemantus, the leisurely approach of Painter and Poet, the soldier's search for the tomb; perhaps there was a vista in the new Italian style of the Court. All plays recalled seem to be indoor pieces; we start with some recollection of Lyly and the first Blackfriars theatre, glance at the bitter comedy of the little eyasses in the second Blackfriars, and end with a grand solo performance for Burbage in the theatre he had owned for more than ten years, but had been prevented from using. It gives him the prominence of the Chief person in a Shew.

Timon's rôle kept the play on the boards in the eighteenth century as vehicle for the great actor managers. A rôle rather than a character, it offered to Richard Burbage special chances to display that Protean variety for which he was renowned. In the masque, Jonson termed Variety 'a principle of the life of these spectacles'; Peacham, in another context said 'It were to draw a picture which should represent all the faces in the world, changing itself like Proteus into all shapes'.[37] The part bears fleeting recollections of many tragic rôles—Hamlet, Lear, Coriolanus, Antony—but Timon is dominated by a succession of moods, each colouring his whole behaviour; so his rôle, in addition to the waterworks, provides a splendid display of histrionic fireworks for his audience. This virtuoso performance, however (contrary to Jonson's masque form) opens with a beautiful House of Fame and ends with 'an ugly hell'.[38]

The strongest evidence that *Timon* was acted lies in the farcial *Comedy of Timon*, with its many comparisons of Timon to Jove, hurling artichokes at the last feast, its use of the Seven Stars as an inn-sign, where a wild drinking party takes place, presenting Timon as king of tosspots till he resigns his 'empire' to a ploughman clown. The Golden Fool Gelasimus' plan for a flight through the Zodiack on Pegasus leaves him cheated of all he has, and he ends digging in a field with the exiled Timon and the faithful steward. Three misanthropists digging in a field is absurd enough even if one of them were not wearing an ass's head, which is eventually bestowed on the philosopher. The sea is not shewn, but is referred to as being just offstage, and Timon offers to Gelasimus 'I'll be thy guide and help thee at a push'. It is unthinkable that the King's Men should take their cues from such a jest; but the lesser always copied the greater, and this little farce makes sense if seen not only as an exercise in Lucian, but as the humble burlesque of a recent grand shew, scenically no less than poetically; for it is obvious that the characters were heavily made up and gaudily dressed, with feathers in their hats, red nose for the usurer, bushy wigs. Then, it becomes immediately recognizable as belonging to a familiar academic tradition, that of *Narcissus*, the play from St John's College, Oxford, which parodies *A Midsummer Night's Dream*; or parts of *Gesta Grayorum*; or for that matter, any Footlights Revue.

What I have suggested, then, is that *Timon* represented Shakespeare's response to the challenge of moving into the new theatre; as a craftsman, though familiar with court shews, he had worked all his life on the great open-air stages. *Timon* would therefore be dated late in 1609 when it was probably staged. What we have is based on the author's manuscript, 'rough work' indeed but not corrupt—partly recopied, and set up, as Hinman tells us, by the wicked Compositor *B*, while the boy prentice distributed the type. Part being recopied by the company's scrivener accounts for some inconsistencies. The indefinite stage directions, as Southern observes, in another respect, could imply that 'conditions under which performance would be given were not specific'[39]—the Blackfriars interior was not settled—and need *not* mean (as Greg imagined) that the play is un-finished. Finally the muddle about the value of the Greek talent, which Spencer made so much of as evidence of revision, can be paralleled in the *Comedy of Timon*, certainly written by a man who knew Greek. I would agree with Honigmann that this is simply a different *kind* of play and not an incomplete draft.[40] And how do we know what ephemera Shakespeare wrote that his friends never pub-lished at all?

In the last decade, the study of Shakespearean produc-tion has undergone a revolution, with the work of Wickham and Southern in England, Jacquot in France, Kernodle, Hosley and Nagler in America. An imaginative knowledge of the live theatre has been turned on the interpretation of the old evidence; and the result is not unlike that by which an archaeologist reconstitutes a lost material culture. It leaves more theoretical study, such as that of Leslie Hotson or Irwin Smith, well behind the present frontiers of know-

ledge, however well documented. A great literary form
like the Revenge Play (which lies behind *Hamlet*) may be
reconstructed from other plays; but this reconstitution of
the theatrical situation may bring about as great a change
in our approach as bibliography did half a century ago, and
disprove Tyrone Guthrie's view that Shakespeare's scenic
tradition was lost when the Globe burnt down in 1613.

What I have suggested about *Timon* makes it into the
work of a theatrical craftsman, in new experimental
approach to an indoor lighted stage. This is Black Vesper's
Pageant. In *Pericles*, which followed, also half spectacle and
half vision, Shakespeare achieved a public success by
concentrating on popular and not courtly spectacle; he also
earned the contempt of Ben Jonson. *The Winter's Tale* is
based on seasonal rhythms, and again the Hero's Protean
moods dominate the scene. In *The Tempest*, vision and shew,
full mastery of form is attained.

Faced with the challenge of new conditions, did the poet
feel, like that later poet, William Yeats, in recalling this
very play, 'Myself I must remake'?[41] If so, we may count
Timon of Athens, in its questing disjunctions, if not Shakespeare's most assured achievement, yet a work of most
heroic endeavour.

NOTES

CHAPTER II

Page   Note No.

4   1.   *Spenser's Images of Life* (1967), p. 3. Spenser's pageants are lost but a line quoted elsewhere as from one of them is found in *F.Q.* II. iii. 25.

4   2.   A. Artaud, tr. M. C. Richards, *The Theatre and Its Double* (1958), p. 89; ibid., p. 44.

6   3.   J. O. Hardison, *Christian Drama and Christian Rite*, Baltimore (1965); V. A. Kolve, *The Play Called Corpus Christi*, Stanford (1966).
Glynne Wickham's *Early English Stages* (1959-   ) is still incomplete.

7   4.   *Le Jeu de la Feuillée* by Adam le Bossu. He was a servant of Robert d'Artois, predecessor of that Robert d'Artois who 78 years later appears in *The Vows of the Heron* (see T. Wright *Political Songs*, vol. 2).

8   5.   Cf. *The Croxton Play of the Sacrament* (*c.* 1461). Compare the Vision with that of Southwell's *The Burning Babe*.

9   6.   Walter Ullmann, *The Individual and Society in the Middle Ages* (1967).

10   7.   See *Malone Society Collections*, VIII (1966), ed. Giles Dawson. The account of the pageant at Canterbury is from this collection.

11   8.   See the article by Sydney Anglo in *Le Lieu théâtral à la Renaissance*, ed. Jean Jacquot (Paris, 1964).

11   9.   C. S. Lewis, *English Literature in the Sixteenth Century* (Oxford, 1954).

12   10.   Christopher Hill, *Reformation to Industrial Revolution* (1967), p. 37.

13   11.   *Lingua* (1605). See however the articles by Patricia Russell and Jocelyn Powell in *Elizabethan Theatre*, Stratford Studies No. 9 (1966).

14   12.   For Elizabeth's monster see her *Englishings*, E.E.T.S. (1889), p. 142 (a translation of Horace).

15   13.   In *English Dramatic Form* (1965), pp. 49-50; also in *Shakespeare's Primitive Art* (Proceedings of the British Academy (1965), pp. 216-7.)

Page Note No.

16 14. Clifford Leech, *The Two Part Play*, Shakespeare Jahrbuch, XCIV (1958), 90-106.

17 15. Nashe, ed. McKerrow, 1, 212; *Piers Pennilesse* (1592).

20 16. The explanations of the Bastard's jealousy of Austria; the Barons' disguise as pilgrims to Bury St Edmunds. It will be seen that I do not accept the theory of the editor of the New Arden edition, that *The Troublesome Reigne* is later than Shakespeare. I think both derive from a third lost play.

24 17. *The Rehearsal*, Act 5 Scene 1 opens with Bayes saying:
Now Gentlemen, I'll shew you the greatest scene that ever England saw; I mean not for words, for those I don't value, but for State, Shew, Magnificence. In fine I'll justify it to be as grand to the eye every whit, I'gad, as that great scene in *Harry* the Eighth, and grander too, I'gad; for instead of two Bishops, I bring in here four cardinals.

25 18. Downes, *Roscius Anglicanus* (1708).

CHAPTER III

30 1. From a lawsuit, for which see C. W. Wallace, *The First London Theatre* (1913).

31 2. For the Great Festival of the Pui, see *Liber Custumarum*, ed. H. T. Riley, *Munimenta Gildhallae Londoniensis*, Rolls Series (London, 1860), vol. 2, part 2, pp. 216-18.

31 3. See *The Rise of the Common Player* (1962), pp. 194-5. A general challenge at wooing is played in Jonson's *Cynthia's Revels*; and in Rowley's *When you See Me, You Know Me*, the jester Will Summers challenges the king to rhyming. (See Chapter IV, p. 49).

33 4. In *The Organization and Personnel of the Shakespearean Company*, (Princeton, 1927). I have set out my views fully in *The Rise of the Common Player* (1962).

34 5. See Sylvia Thrupp, *The Merchant Class and Medieval London* (1300-1500), Michigan, 1962, chapter VI, for a discussion of trade and gentility, and for a study of continental gilds, see Fritz Rörig, *The Medieval Town* (1967). Cf. also below, Chapter V, pp. 88-90.

35 6. A similar incident is shewn in Marston's play *The Phoenix*, IV, 2, 3; it is probably a jest-book story.

NOTES

Page *Note No.*

36   7. Flecknoe, *A Short Discourse of the English Stage* (1664), reprinted in E. K. Chambers, *The Elizabethan Stage* (1924), vol. 4, p. 370.

39   8. See Irwin Smith, 'Theatre into Globe', *Shakespeare Quarterly*, 3.2. (April 1952). (There is still a Curtain Road near Liverpool Street Station in London.)

41   9. See Glynne Wickham, *Early English Stages*, vol. I (1959) p. 248. For a study of the effects of the Blackfriars Theatre on Shakespeare, see Chapter VIII below, and *Shakespeare's Primitive Art*, Proceedings of the British Academy (1965), where I discuss the last plays.

43 10. These 'Sharers' Papers' are reprinted in the *Malone Society Collections*, II, 3.

44 11. See C. J. Sisson, 'The Red Bull Company and the Importunate Widow', *Shakespeare Survey*, vol. 7 (1954); and the Sharers' Papers.

47 12. *A Jovial Crew or The Merry Beggars* had a series of introductory poems praising it, when it appeared in 1652; the Prologue thinks mirth 'a new and forc'd thing in these sad and tragic days . . . jovial mirth is now grown out of fashion', but Alexander Brome, the poet's brother, welcomes the memory of old days.

> Though we have lost their dress, we may be glad
> To see and think on th' happiness we had.

The play remained popular after the Restoration; an opera was made from the play by E. Roome, acted both at Drury Lane and Covent Garden and published in 1780.

CHAPTER IV

49   1. These quotations are from Richard Brome, *The Antipodes*, 2.2.45-8.

51   2. The best account of his life is that by Charles S. Felver, *Robert Armin, Shakespeare's Fool* (Kent State University, Kent, Ohio, Research Series V, 1961).

See also his article on Armin as Touchstone, *S.Q.* VII (1956), 135-7. Armin's life is also discussed by Leslie Hotson in *Shakespeare's Motley* (1952), pp. 84-128.

Page   Note No.

52   3.   *Quips upon Questions* may be treated as one of the minor sources of *Twelfth Night*. It exists in a single imperfect copy in the British Museum, two leaves CI and DI being missing. See T. W. Baldwin *M.L.N.* xxxix (1924), pp. 447-55, who uses it to date *As You Like It*. This work was not previously recognized as Armin's and The Short Title Catalogue ascribed it, for some reason, to John Sharp. Armin's other works were edited by Grosart (1880).

52   4.   *The Praise of Folly* was englished by Sir Thomas Chaloner in 1545 from Erasmus, *Moriae Encomium* of 1511. The world of fools goes back beyond this to Brant's *Ship of Fools* (1494). In France the world of wise fools was associated with law sports and the sottie; see Enid Welsford, *The Fool* (London 1935), part III; and R. H. Goldsmith, *Shakespeare's Wise Fools* Liverpool, 1958). He quotes the mock sermon of Folly in *Ane Satyre of the 3 Estates*, and that of Gelasimus in Grimald's *Archipropheta* (1547) a Latin play.

56   5.   The play belongs to the same tradition as *John a Kent and John a Cumber* and *Friar Bacon and Friar Bungay*; quick changes and magic shews are part of the plots. There seemed to be a convention of the magician and the lovers which can be seen dimly reflected in Armin's very latest work. But *Two Maids of Moreclacke* must have depended almost entirely on Armin's mimicry of Blue-coat John.

59   6.   Leonard Digges in the *Lines* prefixed to *Shakespeare's Poems* (1640):

> Let but Beatrice
> And Benedick be seen, lo in a trice
> The Cockpit, Galleries, Boxes all are full
> To hear Malvolio, that cross garter'd gull.

60   7.   Robert Armin, *Fool upon Fool* (1605), ed. Grosart (1880), pp. 6-7. This violence was due to jealousy; but some masters seem to have tolerated extraordinary ill-behaviour on the part of their household fools, such as the one who stole a special dish for which a large party had been invited, jumped into the moat and stood in the water eating it that he might not be prevented.

61   8.   Malvolio also quotes in all innocence the very dirty little ditty of Richard Tarlton, 'Please one and please all'. He must be presumed not to realize the point of this song which is the same as that of 'A little of what you fancy does you good'.

61   9.   Transmigration denies the resurrection of the body 'So, living in its liberty' adherents 'Commit foul treason, and villainy' (William Rankin, *Seven Satyres*, 1598, p. 17).

62   10.   From the prologue to *Soliman & Perseda* (1590). *The Rare Triumphs of Love and Fortune* shew the two in contest; it was played at Court in 1582 by Derby's Men.

62   11.   Rankin, the academic who wrote *Seven Satyres* against fools (1598) drew Skelton for Henslowe; Rowley's play on Summers is dated 1596; among later fools are Marston's *Passarello* (*The Malcontent*) the fools in *Volpone*, and Babulo in *Patient Grissell*.

William Ferbrand, Armin's printer, also produced *Jack of Dover . . . his quest of Inquirie . . . his privy search for the veriest Fool in England* (1601/1614); a sequel was *The penniless Parliament of threadbare Poets* (1608) published, however, by William Barley.

63   12.   Leslie Hotson connects *Cynthia's Revels* with *Twelfth Night* (*The First Night of Twelfth Night*, 1954), only by way of contrasting its reception and aim. The identification of Jonson with Crites is not accepted by O. J. Campbell (*Comical Satyre*, San Marino, 1938, pp. 82-108).

66   13.   One face, one voice, one habit and two persons

says the Duke (5.i.208).

Do I stand there? I never had a brother
Nor can there be that deity in my nature
Of here and everywhere.

says Sebastian.

69   14.   See B. W. Vickers, '*King Lear* and Renaissance Paradoxes', Modern Language Review (April 1968), vol. 63, No. 2, pp. 305-14.

CHAPTER V

Page   Note No.

76   1. Dryden, *Essay of Dramatic Poesy* (1668); Preface to *Troilus and Cressida* (1679), (*Shakespeare Allusion Book*, Oxford, 1932), 2.144, 246.

76   2. Preface to Oxberry's edition of the play (1820).

78   3. See Sonnet 144, l.12.

79   4. *Shakespeare Allusion Book*, 2.132.

83   5. Greene, *Friar Bacon and Friar Bungay* (*c.* 1589); Houghton's *Englishmen for my Money* (1597); at the same date, Henry Porter's *Two Angry Women of Abingdon*, with its lost sequels; Armin's *Two Maids of Moreclacke* (*c.* 1597); Dekker, *Shoemaker's Holiday* (*c.* 1599); *Wise Woman of Hogsden* (1599); *Merry Devil of Edmonton* (*c.* 1605).

           J. M. Nosworthy's theory that Shakespeare's play was based on a lost play by Porter seems to me untenable, for Porter had written his play for Henslowe and had been paid for it; in what conceivable circumstances would Henslowe allow the rival company to use it? (see *Shakespeare's Occasional Plays*, 1965).

84   6. *Ibid.*, p. 86.

86   7. Ser Giovanni's tale is nearest to Shakespeare; he tells of the undergraduate, who asks his professor to instruct him in the art of love. Unknown to them both, the youth picks on the professor's wife, who first hides him under a pile of washing, secondly between two floor boards, lastly in a pile of deeds in a chest. The enraged professor sets his own house on fire, but has the chest carried out into the woods.

86   8. Perhaps a stock jest in taverns.

87   9. See Richard Bernheimer, *Wild Men in the Middle Ages* (Harvard, 1932).

88   10. See Note 5. Hob the Tanner of Tamworth is in Heywood's *King Edward IV* (1599).

89   11. Jane Austen, Letter to Anna Austen, 14 Sept. 1814.

89   12. Susannah did not marry till she was 24.

91   13. Leslie Hotson, *Shakespeare versus Shallow* (London 1931), discovered that William Gardiner and his nephew William Wayte in November 1596 swore the peace against Shakespeare, Langley of the Swan, and two women; but Langley had just previously sworn the

peace against Wayte and Gardiner. The latter died in November 1597. Hotson dates the play in April 1597 at the Garter feast, but some of the characters come from *Henry V*, which is undoubtedly 1599; and moreover plays like *Eastward Ho!* follow it.

93   14.   It occurs in Brome's *Merry Beggars*, and is probably one of those necessary phrases like 'Marry Trap' which had general currency.

CHAPTER VI

97   1.   The original German is published as Appendix B in T. S. Dorsch's New Arden edition (1955).

98   2.   See Norman Sanders, 'The Shift of Power in *Julius Caesar*', *Review of English Studies* (April 1964), pp. 24-35: 'He was free to consider his theme, political power in its public and personal manifestations, divorced from national allegiances, monarchic preconceptions or any traditional prejudices'.

100   3.   See pp. 33-4 above.

101   4.   See my article, *Shakespeare Quarterly*, IX, 3 (Summer 1958), pp. 311-19.

105   5.   *The Mirror for Magistrates* was the chief transmitter of this doctrine of Fortune; for a general study see Howard Baker, *Induction to Tragedy* (Louisiana, 1939), and Wolfgang Clemen, *English Tragedy Before Shakespeare* (1961).

107   6.   See Howard Patch, *The Goddess Fortune in Medieval Literature* (Cambridge, Mass., 1927), Willard Farnham, *Medieval Heritage of Elizabethan Tragedy*, (Oxford, 1956); Samuel Chew, *Pilgrimage of the Life of Man* (Yale, 1962). Fortune appears in the *Jeu de la Feuillée* (1262), with some of the townsfolk bound upon her wheel.

111   7.   Monica Wilson, *Divine Kings and the Breath of Men*, The Frazer Lecture (1959), pp. 23-4.

116   8.   *Sidney Papers*, ed. A. Collins, ii, 132. Essex's friends commissioned a performance of *Richard II* on the eve of his armed rising.

116   9.   Although *Caesar and Pompey* was not published till 1631, it is usually placed within the years 1606-1611.

Page Note No.

See Millar MacLure, *George Chapman* (Toronto 1966), pp. 151-6). Other plays of these years are William Alexander's *Julius Caesar*, the anonymous *Caesar's Revenge*, both 1607; Samuel Daniel's *Cleopatra* also belongs to this year. Other stoic plays are Fletcher's *Bonduca* and *Valentinian* and *The False One*; Massinger's *Virgin Martyr* and his *Believe as You List*.

118 10. Glynne Wickham, *Early English Stages*, vol. 2, Part I, pp. 4-7.

CHAPTER VII

123 1. Clifford Leech, 'The Dramatist's Independence', *Research Opportunities in Renaissance Drama*, X (1967), p. 19; George Hunter, 'The Heroism of Hamlet' *Hamlet*, Stratford upon Avon Studies 5, ed. B. Harris and J. R. Brown (1963), p. 108.

124 2. *Der Bestrafte Brudermord*, which dates from the early eighteenth century, is translated in the Variorum *Hamlet*. (There is also a German version of *The Spanish Tragedy*.)

125 3. *The Spanish Tragedy*, 3.9.13. The left hand side is the stage side for hell. A similar disposition can be seen in pictorial art, e.g. the frontispiece of Foxe's *Acts and Monuments*.

125 4. James Joyce, *Portrait of the Artist as a Young Man* (1924), pp. 232-3.

125 5. See Howard Baker, *Induction to Tragedy* (Louisiana, 1939); George Hunter, 'Seneca and the Elizabethans', *Shakespeare Survey*, 20 (1967).

126 6. Armin, *A Nest of Ninnies* (1606). The line is not in the present *Hamlet*; but cf. the additions to *The Spanish Tragedy* Third Addition, 11.41-2.

Well, heaven is heaven still,
And there is Nemesis and Furies,
And things call'd whips.

(whips being carried by these characters).

126 7. Milton, *First Elegy*, written to Charles Diodati 'Sive cruentatum furiosa Tragoedia sceptrum. Quasset et effusa crinibus ora rota . . .'. This kind of language

Page   Note No.

appears in *Mulleasses the Turk* (1607) and later 'Turkish' plays.

128   8.   George Hunter, Preface to *Antonio and Mellida* (Regents Renaissance Drama, 1965), p. xviii.

129   9.   See above, Chapter III, p. 36.

130   10.   Betterton (here described) had learnt from Davenant who learnt from Taylor, 'who was instructed by Mr Shakespeare himself' as Downes states in his *Roscius Anglicanus* (1708). It appears that the author sometimes acted as director, and Hamlet's instructions to the player which were remembered by Dick Brome in his *Antipodes* (see above, Chapter III) may represent something of the dramatist's own principles.

131   11.   The quotations in this paragraph are from Brian Gibbons, *The Jacobean City Comedy* (1968), p. 98; and from Beaumont's play, *The Woman Hater* (Prologue), (1606). For the date of *The Malcontent* see the preface to Bernard Harris's edition (New Mermaid, Benn, 1967). For the relation of *Antonio's Revenge* to *Hamlet*, see the article by Smith and Kaufman, *Shakespeare Quarterly*, ix, 4 (Autumn, 1958), pp. 493ff.

133   12.   'Thou antic death which laugh'st us here to scorn' (*I Henry VI*, 4.7.18) 'Within the hollow crown.... Keeps Death his court and there the antic sits' (*Richard II*, 3.2.160) seem to be derived from Holbein's *Dance of Death*. The witless antics, Distraction, Frenzy and Amazement appear in *Troilus and Cressida*, 5.3.86. In *Love's Labour's Lost* the country people plan that if their shew does not 'fadge' they will have an 'antic' and on Pompey's galley Caesar says 'The wild disguise hath almost antick'd us all'. The most pathetic use of the term comes in Calantha's death scene in Ford's *Broken Heart*:

> I but deceiv'd your eyes with antic gesture,
> When one news straight came huddled on another
> Of death and death and death, still I danc'd forward.

133   13.   The actors did not take the point, for in the Bad Quarto, Hamlet does address Claudius as Father on a number of occasions.

134   14.   From 'angels and ministers of Grace defend us!' to the ghost's description of Lewdness courting Virtue in the

'shape of a radiant angel' to Hamlet's invocation of St Patrick' said against the 'serpent' that did sting his father's life there is a continuous stream of imagery in Act I; the most notable of course is the account of the disappearance of 'spirits' at Christmas. Angelic imagery is associated with Ophelia throughout, to Laertes' final words over her grave, but emotively, not with 'weight'. Hamlet's impulse to send Claudius to hell is also an emotive explosion, roused by the sight of him in his struggling prayer.

136 15. These lines, and the acceptance of Providence, with the qualms of natural dread appear only in the latest version.

137 16. The boys danced and sang between the acts; there was a preliminary concert of music at Blackfriars. But the personal references whether of compliment or detraction were not taken over from the private theatres, although the new realistic kind of acting in comedy made everyone tend to think that the characters were drawn from life.

137 17. Anthony Copley dedicated *A Fig for Fortune* to Anthony Browne, Lord Montague, Southampton's cousin. He was himself educated at the Inns of Court, but went abroad in 1582, served Spain, visited Rome, was imprisoned on his return for a time. In 1603 he was condemned to death for supporting Arabella Stuart's claims to the throne; after his pardon he went abroad and nothing is heard of him after 1607.

141 18. As given by the Czech Theatre of the Balustrade in 1968, the play became a political satire, quite in the Elizabethan manner; but the young Prince was very clearly dressed and presented as a Hamlet-figure, in parody (the ghosts handed him a sword).

CHAPTER VIII

144   1. Nashe, *Summer's Last Will and Testament*, ed. McKerrow, Vol. III, *Prol.* l. 75.

145   2. Masque at the wedding of Sir Philip Herbert and Lady Susan Vere (see Enid Welsford, *The Court Masque*, 1927, p. 173).

145   3. Cf. also the two graces, of Apemantus and Timon (1.1. 198-200, cf. 5.1.30-1; 1.1.189-90, cf. 4.3.278-9).

NOTES

Page *Note No.*

146 4. *A Natural Perspective* (1965), p. 98.

146 5. Clifford Leech, *Shakespeare's Tragedies* (1950), p. 124; cf. John Wain, *The Living World of Shakespeare* (1963); Wilson Knight's essay appeared in *The Wheel of Fire* (1930).

147 6. L. Wager, *Enough is as good as a Feast* (c. 1564).

147 7. *Philanthropy in England*, 1480-1660 (1959), pp. 265-74.

147 8. Robert Wilson, *Three Ladies of London* (c. 1583), a play of the Queen's men.

148 9. Fortune is the daughter of Plutus in *The Rare Triumphs of Love and Fortune*. For other treatments of Fortune see *Liberality and Prodigality*, c. 1565, revived 1602; Lupton's *All for Money*; Dekker's *Old Fortunatus*; Middleton's *Hengist King of Kent*. The four craftsmen at first meet a fifth, the Mercer; this will in fact be the particular rôle for the Merchant; he was a traditional follower of all prodigals, as in Middleton's *Michaelmas Term*, referred to below (Note 19). The speech-heading 'Mer.' conflates the rôles.

148 10. 'Greeks and Merrygreeks, a Background to *Timon of Athens* and *Troilus and Cressida*', in *Essays on Shakespeare and Elizabethan Drama in honour of Hardin Craig*, ed. Richard Hosley, University of Missouri Press, 1962.

148 11. North's *Plutarch* (Nonesuch Press ed., 1929), I, 369.

149 12. Cf. 'Such Lords eat men but men shall eat up me' (the bountiful Gentili in Dekker's *Wonder of a Kingdom*, 4.1.70). This play seems in many ways to recall *Timon*, in its contrast of liberality and prodigality

149 13. Cupid could move about blindfold, as T. W. Craik notes of other characters (*Tudor Interlude*, 1958, p. 63) more particularly of course Fortune.

150 14. 5.1.92-110; cf. also Middleton *The Changeling*, 1.2.181-203, for a riddling game about knaves and fools.

150 15. It was edited for the Shakespeare Society by A. Dyce in 1842. The Epilogue terms it a 'comedy and merry scene'. Pegasus (see p. 165) is the badge of the Inner Temple. I have written on this play in *Renaissance Drama*, 8, (1967).

150 16. Gelasimus is a character in Nicholas Grimald's Latin play *Archipropheta* (1547).

179

Page Note No.

152 17. E.g. Wilson's *The Cobbler's Prophecy* contains such a soldier; so does Skelton's *Magnyfycence*.

152 18. *Liberality and Prodigality*, 3. 3. Prodigality and Money 'Exeunt. Flie gold-knaps' (or buttercups). Cf. Ceres strewing sweetmeats in Wilson's *Cobbler's Prophecy*, and for medieval feasts see Glynne Wickham, *Early English Stages* (1959), I, p. 95.

154 19. Such for instance as *Eastward Ho!* a parody of the usual prodigal play, and Middleton's *Michaelmas Term*. In earlier works, e.g. the character of Asper in *Every Man out of his Humour*, Jonson took a line much nearer to Apemantus. For a character successively ruled by different humours, cf. Pandora, the Heroine of Lyly's comedy *The Woman in the Moon*. Timon has other echoes of Lyly, e.g. the cynic Diogenes of *Campaspe* seems to anticipate Apemantus. Lyly's plays had been staged at Blackfriars in the eighties, Jonson's c. 1602-5.

154 20. Definitions of the shew may be gathered from Jonson, e.g. 'The nature and property of these devices being to present always some one entire body or figure, consisting of distinct members and each of those expressing itself, . . . yet so composed and disposed, as no one little part can be missing to the illustration of the whole' (Pamphlet on King James's welcome, 1604). 'A principle of the life of such spectacles lies in their variety' (*Masque of Fame*, 1609).

155 21. Cf. 2.2.177-8, 3.6.30, 4.3.264-6. The beast imagery has been often discussed.

155 22. Used as a school test in Erasmus' translation; printed in the New Arden edition as an appendix, The *Comedy of Timon* was composed from Lucian but with recollections of Shakespeare.

155 23. See G. Baldini, *Manualetto Shakespeariano* (1964), p. 462.

156 24. The Four Seasons appear in the masque noted on p. 178, n. 2, Fame and the Five Senses in *Nova Felix Arabia* (1604) in the coronation entry of James I. The Four Humours appear in Jonson's *Hymenai* and the Twelve Signs of the Zodiac in his *Masque of Cupid*; they were the commonplaces of masquing. Middleton has the days of the week in one masque.

NOTES

Page *Note No.*

157 25. Montaigne, translated by Florio, *Essays*, The First Book, chapter LI; 'Of Democritus and Heraclitus'. Shakespeare had evidently read this passage on Timon.

157 26. Apemantus appears in Plutarch's life of Mark Antony as a friend of Timon, and of a like humour (Nonesuch ed., vol. IV, p. 348).

158 27. It is hardly necessary to refer to the great lines in *Macbeth* uniting pity and tears (1.7.21-5). Dekker's pageant is *Nova Felix Arabia* (ed. Bowers, vol. 2, p. 276).

158 28. 2 Cor. vi. 9-10: Epistle for the first Sunday in Lent.

159 29. The year ended with the 24th of March (Old Style).

159 30. Peter Laslett, *The World we have Lost* (1965), p. 126.

161 31. Also *Lusty Juventus, Misogonus, Nice Wanton*. Marlowe's Faustus is tempted by poison, guns, halters and venom'd steel (ll. 629-36) to commit suicide.

161 32. See Susan Snyder, 'The left hand of God; Despair in Medieval and Renaissance Tradition', *Studies in the Renaissance*, XII (1965), 18-59.

163 33. Cf. A. M. Nagler, *Theatre Festivals of the Medici 1537-1632* (1964), and also the article by Glynne Wickham in *Le Lieu Théâtral à la Renaissance* (Paris, 1964), ed. Jean Jacquot, which suggests that political reasons kept Italian influence from the English stage until the accession of James I.

163 34. Irwin Smith, *Shakespeare's Blackfriars Playhouse* (1966), p. 232.

163 35. J. M. Nosworthy, *Shakespeare's Occasional Plays* (1965), p. 225. See also the article by E. A. J. Honigmann, *Shakespeare Quarterly*, XII, 1 (Winter, 1961), 3-20, which argues that *Timon* was intended for the Inns of Court, and links it to *Antony and Cleopatra*.

164 36. In the well-known collection of masque music, B.M. Add. 10444. For an account of music see J. P. Cutts, *La Musique de scène de la troupe Shakespearienne* (Paris, 1959); F. W. Sternfeld, *Music in Shakespearean Tragedy* (1963); and Andrew J. Sabol, *Songs and Dances for the Stuart Masque* (Brown University Press, 1959), who prints extracts from the manuscript.

165 37. H. Peacham, *The Compleat Gentleman* (1622), Chapter X.

SHAKESPEARE THE CRAFTSMAN

165 38. The disposition of Jonson, *Masque of Fame* which had an antemasque of hell; *Timon* seems to reverse this usual order.

166 39. See the article by Richard Southern in the volume edited by Richard Hosley and cited in Note 10, p. 179.

166 40. See article cited in Note 35. For Spencer, see 'Shakespeare learns the value of money', *Shakespeare Survey* 6 (1953).

167 41. William Yeats, 'An Acre of Grass' (*Last Poems*). I cannot but think that the great epitaph of Yeats, as he lies by the shore at Drumcliffe, owes something to Timon's epitaph: 'Pass, and stay not here thy gait . . .' 'Horseman, pass by'.

INDEX

(Plays, except Shakespeare's, appear under the author or town of origin)

Alleyn, E., 29, 31, 36, 42, 72, 125

All's Well, 50

Anglo, S., 169

Anne (of Denmark), Queen, 118, 163

Antony and Cleopatra, 68, 116, 117-21

Apius and Virginia, 35-6

Armin, R., 23, 49-74, 126, 135; *Fool upon Fool*, 70; *Two Maids of Moreclacke*, 56-7, 70; *Valiant Welshman*, 71

Armstrong, Archy, 73

Arras, *Jeu de la Feuillée*, 6-7

Artaud, A., 4

As You Like It, 55, 59, 80

Auden, W. H., 75

Austen, Jane, 89

Bacon, F., 101, 125, 158

Baldwin, T. W., 33, 172

Bale, J., 12; *King Johan*, 18, 36

Beaumont, F., *Knight of the Burning Pestle*, 19, 41

Becket, St Thomas, Play of, 11

Beeston, W., 44

Betterton, T., 25, 130

Blackfriars Theatre, 2, 23, 26, 37, 40, 42-3, 129, 163-7, 171

Brayne, E., 28-9

Brome, R., 2, 44-9; *The Antipodes*, 44-6, 177; *A Jovial Crew*, 46-8

Buckingham, Dukes of, 24, 25

Burbage, C., 27, 38, 42-3

Burbage, J., 27-30, 35, 38

Burbage, R., 19, 27, 29-30, 35, 38, 40-2, 96, 129-30, 131, 135, 160, 164, 165

Campbell, O. J., 173

Cardenio, 31

Cartwright, W., *Verses on Fletcher*, 62

Caxton, W., *Game and Play at Chesse*, 12

Chandois, Lady M., 67, 70

Chandois, Lord, 52, 70

Chapman, G., *Caesar and Pompey*, 116; McLure, M., *George Chapman*, 174

Charles I, King, 48, 59, 62

Chaucer, G., 82, 101, 107, 108

Chettle, H., *Hoffman*, 132

Christmas Prince, 73

Condell, H., 26, 41, 42, 130-1

Conrad, J., 121

Cook, A. B., *Zeus*, 153

Copley, A., *A Fig for Fortune*, 137-8

Coriolanus, 4, 98, 100, 116-17

Coventry Play, 9

Curtain Theatre, 29, 39, 52

Davies, J. of Hereford, *Scourge of Folly*, 30, 35, 73

Dekker, T., 33, 41, 44, 92, 174, 179, 181; *Sun's Darling*, 161-3
Digges, L., 114, 172
Downes, J., *Roscius Anglicanus*, 170, 177
Dryden, J., 75-6

Eliot, T. S., *Burnt Norton*, 156
Elizabeth I, Queen, 9, 14, 18, 23, 37, 76-7, 92-3, 115, 137-8
Elizabeth of Bohemia, Queen, 22-3
Elton, G., 118
Erasmus, *Praise of Folly*, 52, 54, 60, 63, 69
Essex, Earl of, 115, 175

Ferbrand, W., 62, 173
Fiorentino, G., 85, 174
Flecknoe, Richard, 171
Ford, J., *Broken Heart*, 177; *Sun's Darling, see* Dekker
Foxe, J., *Acts and Monuments*, 15, 18, 24, 176
Frye, N., 146

Gardiner, Judge, 91-2, 174-5
Garzoni, T., *Hospital of Incurable Fools*, 62-3
Gascon, J., 94
Gibbon, B., *Jacobean City Comedy*, 132, 177
Gilbert, W. S., *Rosencrantz and Guildenstern*, 140
Globe, Theatre, 26, 39, 41, 59, 71, 97, 99, 163, 164
Greene, R., 14-15, 46; *Friar*

Bacon, 82, 172; *Looking Glass for London*, 161

Hall, Dr John, 81, 89
Hamblet, *Hystorie of*, 123, 132
Hamlet, 1-2, 13, 37-8, 44, 46, 50, 54, 109, 122-39, 164
Hamlet Travestie, 140
Hardison, J. O., 6, 22
Heminges, J., 26, 41, 42, 43
Henry IV, 22
Henry V, 1, 22, 77, 78, 108, 175
Henry VI, 16, 17, 113, 177
Henry VIII, 9, 22-6, 41
Henry VIII, King, 11, 24
Henslowe, P., 30, 36, 132
Herbert, Sir W., 43
Heron, *Vows of the*, 4
Heywood, T., 41, *Apology for Actors*, 160; *Edward IV*, 22; *The English Traveller*, 41
Hill, C., 33, 169
Hinman, C., 166
Holbein, H., 11, 59, 177
Honigmann, E., 166
Hopkins, G. M., 139
Hotson, L., 67, 77, 91, 171, 173, 174-5
Hunsdon, Baron, 30, 37
Hunter, G., 176, 177

James I, King, 5, 39, 73, 158, 180
Jarry, A., *Ubu Roi*, 140-1
John, King, 16-22
Johnson, S., 88, 130
Jonson, B., 44, 60, 92, 96, 104, 114, 154, 163, 165, 180,

INDEX

182; *Blackness, Masque of,* 118; *Cynthia's Revels,* 63, 170, 173; *Eastward Ho!,* 55, 180; *Fame, Masque of,* 180, 182
Jordan, W. K., 147
Julius Caesar, 35, 97-116

Keats, J., 158
Kempe, W., 49-50; *Knack to Know a Knave,* 49
Kentish plays, 10
Kernodle, G. R., 99, 166
Klibansky, R., *Saturn and Melancholy,* 155
Kolve, V. A., 6, 7
Kyd, T., 123, 124-8; *The Spanish Tragedy,* 124-5

Lear, King, 50, 59, 67, 68-9
Leech, C., 16, 176, 179
Leicester, Earl of, 28, 30, 45
Levin, H., 139
Lewis, C. S., 4, 169
Liberality and Prodigality, 146, 180
Lingua, 169
Love's Labour's Lost, 32-3, 49, 77, 96, 158, 177
Lowin, J., 23, 25, 42, 131
Lucian, *Timon,* 149, 155
Lucy, Sir T., 91
Lydgate, J., 79
Lyly, J., 31, 164, 180; *Euphues,* 36

Macbeth, 5-6, 68, 181
Machiavelli, N., 86
Manningham's Diary, 35

Marlowe, C., *Faustus,* 181; *Massacre at Paris,* 18; *Tamburlaine,* 15, 16, 107
Marston, J., 111, 116; *Antonio's Revenge,* 127-9, 177; *The Malcontent,* 130-2; *The Phoenix,* 170; *Eastward Ho!, see* Jonson B
Merchant of Venice, 109
Merry Wives of Windsor, 75-96
Middleton, T., 12; *Hengist King of Kent,* 73, 179
Midsummer Night's Dream, 67, 77, 92, 166
Miller, J., 70
Milton, J., 126
Mirk, J., 8
Mirror for Magistrates, The, 175
Montaigne, M. de, 157, 181
More, St Thomas, 52
More, Sir Thomas, 13, 113
Much Ado, 50

Narcissus, 166
Nashe, T., 17, 24; *Summer's Last Will,* 162-3
Newcastle, Duchess of, 79
Nosworthy, J. M., 163, 174, 181

Oxberry, W., 76

Panovsky, E., *see* Klibansky R.
Peacham, G., 165
Peele, G., 66; *King Edward I,* 13-14, 17; *Merry Jests,* 93
Percy, Sir C., 84

Pericles, 31, 167
Pico della Mirandola, 107
Plutarch, 104, 131, 148, 181
Pui, Gild of, 31
Puttenham, G., 12, 35

Ralegh, Sir W., 107
Rankin, W., Seven Satyres, 173
Rape of Lucrece, 98
Rare Triumphs of Love and Fortune, 173, 179
Red Bull Theatre, 22, 43
Reddaway, T. F., 33, 100
Richard II, 59, 102, 164, 175, 177
Richard III, 102, 124
Richards, I. A., 103
Romeo and Juliet, 38, 50, 75, 108
Rörig, F., Medieval Town, 170
Rowley, W., When You See Me, 49, 170
Rutland, Earl of, 33, 40, 116

Sanders, N., 175
Sartre, J.-P., 122
Saxl, F., see Klibansky
Shanks, J., 43
Shaw, G. B., 88, 101
Shirley, J., 41, 46
Sisson, C. J., 171
Skelton, J., Magnyfycence, 137, 161, 180
Smith, I., 171, 181
Sonnets, 31-3, 90, 134, 148
Southampton, Earl of, 17, 31, 84, 115
Spanish popular plays, 7-8

Spencer, T., 148
Spenser, E., 31; Faerie Queene, 4, 110, 138, 161
Stoppard, T., Rosencrantz and Guildenstern are Dead, 140, 141-3
Straparola, G., Piacevoli Notti, 57, 71, 85

Taming of the Shrew, 13, 47
Tarlton, R., 17, 49, 51, 53, 54, 86, 135, 173
Theatre, Shoreditch, 28-30, 36, 38, 97
Three Lords and Three Ladies of London, 54
Thrupp, S., The Merchant Class of Medieval London, 170
Timon, Comedy of, 150, 152, 160, 165
Timon of Athens, 98, 144-67
Titus Andronicus, 33, 98, 126
Troilus and Cressida, 1, 100-1, 102, 177
Troublesome Reign of King John, The, 18-19
Twelfth Night, 54, 56, 57-67, 78
Two Angry Women of Abingdon, 174
Two Merry Women of Abingdon, 95

Ullmann, W., 9, 11

Van Doran, M., 59
Venus and Adonis, 31, 34
Verdi, G., 77
Vickers, B. W., 173

INDEX

Wain, J., 179

Webster, J., 111, 116

Welsford, E., 172, 178

Wickham, G., 6, 118, 181

Wilson, F. P., 103

Wilson, M. M., 111

Wilson, R., *Three Ladies of London*, 179; *Cobbler's Prophecy*, 180; *see also* under *Three Lords and Three Ladies of London*

Winter's Tale, The, 23, 167

Wotton, Sir H., 24, 25

Württemburg, Duke of, 91, 94

Yeats, W. B., 141, 167, 182